LIVING IN THE KEY OF

JOY

*Personal stories to inspire
you to paint your own
picture of happiness and joy*

D1282360

PRESENTED BY
GAIL CLANTON

Copyright © 2022 by Clanton Communications, LLC

Cover design by Janet Harward, JanetDesign
janetharward.myportfolio.com

ISBN 978-0-578-37974-6

Table Of Contents

Dedication

I dedicate this book to the memory
of my dear sisterfriend,
Suzanne Lynn "Free" Anderson.

I am ever so grateful for the many years of
JOY we shared, and I rejoice in knowing that
she is now totally and completely Free.

Forward

Joy is not a reaction to what happens around you; rather joy is a way of living based upon what happens within.

As the authors in this volume share with you…

Joy keeps you strong and grounded and fuels new beginnings.

Joy opens our eyes – literally and figuratively – to see the beauty and opportunities around us.

Joy can surprise you and show up when you least expect it, in a manner that you least expect.

Joy sparkles brightest when given away.

We hope that reading the stories in this collection will inspire you to color your world with your own unique brand of joy. Take the paint brush and just go wild; then share that joy with someone else. Let's help create a world that allows us to live together peacefully and harmoniously… **In the Key of Joy.**

Gail Clanton

Project Presenter

Praying, Planning, Pivoting and Prospering

Diane Ables

Praying, Planning, Pivoting and Prospering

Diane Ables

"For I Know the plans I have for you, declares the Lord, plans to prosper you and not to harm you, plans to give you hope and a future" - Jeremiah 29:11 NIV

*I acknowledge all the unconditional love and support from my deceased mom, **Marian Moseley Price**, Gail Clanton, the visionary for this book, the other writers, my family and loved ones. Finally, I have the greatest appreciation for three phenomenal women who have transitioned in the past two years: my beloved cousin, Sandra B. Hamilton, Reverend Sheila H. Bradshaw, and Lynne B. Collins, aka, Mama Nzingha. May their souls rest in peace.*

Today, at 77 years young, I ask myself "How I am going to spend the next chapter in my life?" I have purposely identified four tools for my growth and development during this season and I'll share them with you now:

Praying In his book "The Purpose Driven Life", Rick Warren states "If you want to know why you were placed on this planet, you must begin with God." Prayer is the foundation of my life and I believe and trust that God does everything in HIS own time. I know this is real because of all my experiences with the deaths of loved ones, car accidents, and so many other difficult events. While not what I would have wanted, I know that those events were divinely orchestrated and I'm grateful that God sustained me through them all. But I had to put in some work. Faith requires action, for faith without works is like "a cart without a horse".

My prayer life is centered around reading Scriptures and surrounding myself with fellow believers. I pray for world peace, the sick, the homeless, and victims of senseless crimes. This pandemic is beyond human comprehension. Yet, I know that prayer is the answer and that all things work together for believers.

Planning involves focusing and prioritizing my goals by writing them down. I enjoy writing stories, keeping a journal, and writing letters. These writings hold me accountable to making good choices and following through. I also seek relationships with positive people who will hold me accountable as I seek excellence rather than perfection!

In this area of my life, I work toward my four D's: **dedication, diligence, determination, and discernment**. My short-term plans include continuing to write, sticking to a structured exercise plan, and remodeling my home. I also plan to continue my volunteer work with non-profits that support victims of domestic violence and single parents. My long-term plans are to travel (once the current restrictions are lifted), to become a world-class Christian, and I want to laugh more and worry less. I know this life is not a dress rehearsal.

If you're like me, you may find it easy to get distracted when planning to reach your goals. (That's another "D" word!) For me, the distraction has been social media, and it can get in the way of my planning and living a balanced life. I saw something recently about how using social media and our cell phones to connect with those far away stops us from being connected with those close to us. I think that's true, and I often wonder what life would be like if there were no cell phones, television, or computers. Back in my day we had none of those things and we survived!

Pivoting We all know about Murphy's Law, that anything that can go wrong will go wrong. Oh yes, I know this is so real. I think about the numerous times I had what I thought was the perfect plan and the unexpected has happened.

For example, I am currently substitute teaching at the elementary school level. The regular teacher has left well-organized plans and classwork. Now this sounds great, but no, that has not been the case. I am often challenged with students who do not accept my role as their substitute teacher and just don't want to do the work as assigned. As a result, I have to be very creative, while still adhering to the assigned classwork. I've shifted the assignment slightly to have students write a story about their family or about fun things they like to do. We then have "show and tell" time. This has been a major pivot for them and for me. The students learn to think creatively and accept a change in the everyday teaching and learning experiences. And I am mastering the concept of pivoting with The Serenity Prayer as my mantra "God grant me the serenity to accept the things that I cannot change, the courage to change the things I can and **the wisdom to know the difference."**

Prospering My greatest reward in life comes from embracing the fruits of the spirit: **love, joy, peace, patience, kindness, generosity, faithfulness, gentleness, and self-control.** In our fast-paced world of materialistic values, homes, cars, jobs (which can all be taken away as quickly as they were acquired) many people are not focusing on good health, helping others to see the light, smiling, or giving someone something to smile about. At this point in my life, these latter things mean more to me than having a large amount of money. Have I always felt this way? The answer is **NO.** Yet, God's grace and mercy have favored me to now value the substance of these things. Yes, I do need money to live a comfortable lifestyle and that is okay. Yet, I know without a doubt that my health is my wealth.

Another thing that is allowing me to prosper is my willingness to ask for help. This is not a sign of weakness but a sign that another person can and will give me unconditional support. This provides us both with a win.

In closing, my life and legacy for generations to come will be to live, laugh, and love.

Love Fulfilled My Joy

Reverend Claudette Abney

Love Fulfilled My Joy

Reverend Claudette Abney

Today, my life suddenly changed.

Everything got rearranged
Into something I cannot explain, except to say
that I am in great pain.
My body trembles, my eyes tear, my soul weeps,
my heart fears.
The choice of what to do or where to go, as well as the when, I do
not know.
My mind stumbles, my feet slip, my knees wobble, my hands lose
their grip.
What direction to take seems hidden from view and I cannot tell
which course to pursue.

My ears grow deaf and I am numb; my spirit never sleeps, waiting
for the answer to come.

I cry ... and cry ... and cry ... and cry, hoping to answer the
question why
My life suddenly changed, why everything got rearranged
So that ...I Feel -- NO LONGER ME!

How does one prepare for something so unexpected? In the prime of my life, Autumn decided to show up. In a moment, one flickering second, the weather inside my body drastically changed and

I found myself in the middle of unwelcomed physical instability and uncertainty. Things suddenly changed and life became colorful; but, not in a good way. None of this was pretty like the changing of the leaves in Autumn some of us so greatly admire. This season is usually marked by pleasant cooler temperatures. But, this was starting to feel cold. The climate conditions in my life went from Summer to Fall without warning, in the twinkling of an eye, no transition stage.

Autumn is supposed to be harvest time, a time of gathering. I was experiencing nothing but loss and, when the fruit finally started coming in, it amounted to discomfort 24 hours a day, seven days a week, by way of aching joints, an elevated fever, fatigue that could make anyone lose their mind and an ugly rash right across the face, the place of outward recognition. This was not the way harvest is supposed to work. This was agony. This was lupus erythematosus, a systemic autoimmune disease which attacks the immune system due to an internal misunderstanding, wherein the body thinks it is being invaded by a destructive intruder and goes on the attack. There is no intruder; so, the body ends up attacking itself.

The loss is considerable. Your health anchors your life and when you lose it, it can take with it your ability to earn an income. Now, the questions become: "How will I eat? Where will I live? How will I clothe myself? How will I pay for all these medications and hundreds of thousands of dollars in medical bills?" These are not even the biggest questions. The question looming largest and overshadowing everything was: "How will I stay alive?" This is my journey through the roadblock called lupus to the place of love and joy.

I was thirty-nine years old and totally disabled. Thirty-nine trying to figure out how not to die. I cannot begin to tell you the emotional and psychological effect this takes on a person, knowing you are being tortured by yourself, by your own body. The knowledge that your own body has rejected you, through no fault of your own, is hard to wrap your mind around. The loss continued relentlessly. With loss comes grief. Loss, of any kind, is a type of death. Not only did I have the grief of losing the function of my body, but I also had to endure the loss of friendships and relationships. When your life changes, so do the people in your life. People began to walk out of my life. They do not have time for the abnormal person. This is a world where normal reigns, whatever that is.

Any sign of difference and you are out, especially a sign of illness because that is seen as weakness. Though I was disappointed by this loss as well, I had to understand that some people are just not suitable for your journey. Not everyone can go with you, nor should they. People also reject what they do not understand. I had family and friends; but, they had struggles of their own. Yes, I could talk to them; but, I could not ask anyone to support me beyond occasional emotional support. I was an adult, and this was totally my responsibility, my burden to bear.

The greatest loss in all of this was choosing to birth no children. The weight of this decision was so heavy that I thought I would break beneath it. It was, however, the right decision for me. I could not care for children with this disease incapacitating me day and night. During this precious time, as I was nearing the end of my childbearing years, I was bedbound. I had no way to support children. Children must eat and they must have a safe and comfortable home. Children need to be clothed and educated, and they need someone who is emotionally, mentally and physically available. I was not. I was busy saving my life.

Since I am a firm believer that one should not have children they cannot care for, I made the courageous and loving decision to have no offspring. My legacy would have to be something else.

Now, I have empty arms, another burden, another loss, though this time it was love's choice. Lonely does not even begin to explain this experience. There are just no words to convey my heart's pain and sadness. Not only was the life I spent so much time and effort prayerfully planning not going to be, but it appeared nothing was going to be -- not even me. Everything deconstructed at the same time, my faith included. If God is omniscient, why didn't God give me a head's up about what was coming? Would this not have been the kind thing to do? Even more, since God is all powerful, why didn't God just stop this from occurring? This truly was my dark night of the soul.

And then, suddenly, I perceived God again, I touched God again. Despite all this torment, I sensed a calling, a mission of sorts, in this wilderness. I began to understand that the unseen blessing in this Autumn, is that Autumn still knows that Spring will come again, no matter what stands between them. Allowing this thought to take over my mind, led to an upward turn in the way I viewed my circumstances. I was no longer looking for happiness based on circumstances. I was in search of joy. Autumn had come to remind me of life's transitoriness and how important it is to find joy amid Autumnal changes. As Autumn's colors continue to manifest themselves, I see its beautiful colors again and I catch a glimpse of light from The Bible, the Holy Scriptures of Christianity, that give me the audacity to have hope, the kind of hope that makes one not ashamed that you believe. "Hope does not put us to shame because God's love has been poured out into our hearts through the Holy Spirit. We do not hope in vain because, even in this life, we have benefits in Christ, such as the LOVE that God puts into us" (Rom. 5:5).

There it was. LOVE. This wilderness is about love. I reimagined the Holy Scriptures in my life and situation as I read "The entrance of thy Word gives light and understanding" (Ps. 119:130) and "Thy Word is a lamp unto my feet and a light unto my path" (Ps. 119:105). October's colors become more vibrant and further light enters my soul as I read "Remember how the Lord your God led you all the way in the wilderness...to teach you that one does not live on bread alone but by every word that comes from the mouth of God" (Deut. 8:2-3). Love is bringing me to a sure place where I know that "God's Word will not return empty. It will accomplish what God desires and achieve the purpose for which God sent it" (Is. 55:11). More hues of hope appear as I read the words of Elkanah (EL means God) to his wife Hannah who is despondent because she has not given birth to a child. "Hannah, why do you weep and why do you not eat and why is your heart sad? Am I not better to you than ten sons?" (I Sam.1:8). Not only was he telling his wife that he would love her even if she never gave birth, but the Scripture records also that Elkanah gave Hannah a double portion of his earthly goods (Sam. 1:5). This portion was normally the firstborn son's inheritance only (Deut. 21:17). But Elkanah gave the firstborn's inheritance to the barren Hannah because he loved her.

Despite not being able to work since age thirty-nine (I am now sixty-four) and bearing no children, God (Elkanah) has given to me a double portion. As it says in Ps. 23:1 "Because the Lord is my Shepherd, I have everything I need." I lack for nothing. I own a home that is more than enough to meet my needs. The pantry is filled and I cannot get another thing in the freezer. God places upon the heart of a local pastor to call periodically to make sure I have enough to eat. God, indeed, has been better to me than ten sons. Once again, a beautiful color appears in October as I ponder my good fortune and I see the words "Give and it will be given to you. A good measure, pressed down, shaken together and running over, will be poured into your lap. For with the measure you use, it will be measured to you" (Luke 6:38). Although I was barely alive, I continued to give to the best of my ability to those in need and God did not forget my labor of love toward His people. This wilderness is about love, no matter what happens.

Has the loss ceased? No. Deconstruction and reconstruction is a lifelong process, as we go from glory to glory. The glory of my Autumn has been love, God's love for me. God was in it all along, guiding and sustaining. I learned to love myself more, to be kind and gentle with myself and to give the same compassion to myself that I give to others. I love myself by understanding that acceptance of my situation does not mean defeat. It means not being in denial and working with what is. What remains is enough. So am I. I have chosen to love and embrace my limitations. They have opened doors to new possibilities and restoration of gifts that had been lying dormant within me. Love taught me that I still have something to offer. When others choose to cut me off from human relationship, I am still accepted by God in the Beloved, Christ Jesus, and always will be. You will be, too. It is the love of God and for God, as well as the love of self and others that fulfills my joy.

My life remains in Autumn with mixed colors presenting themselves in varied intensities and values. But, as I look ahead to Winter, the fears, the doubts and the loneliness have dissipated. Because of God, who is love itself, I can conquer anything. Love will fulfill my joy in every season of life, and I think I see a warm December just over the horizon.

.

Joy Found Through Lifetime Scars

Dr. Nialah Ali

Joy Found Through Lifetime Scars

Dr. Nialah Ali

The definition of a scar is a mark left on the skin after it heals or a sign of mental or physical damage. It is the lasting mental or emotional effects of suffering anguish and speaks to the act of leaving lasting signs of damage.

Throughout our lifetimes we will experience scars either physically, mentally, or emotionally. One may ask "What should we do when we get these scars?" Let me tell you my story of how I turned my inward and outward scars into triumphant signs of joy.

Buster Brown Shoes

Kingsman Elementary was right around the corner from our house. My siblings and I could walk to school, and we came home every day for lunch. I remember on those snowy days, Momma would have a warm bowl of tomato soup, with a bologna and cheese sandwich waiting for us. That bowl of soup kept us warm for that walk back to school.

One day when I got back after lunch, someone had drawn a picture of my shoes, and it included images of crushed grass and dirt. The picture was titled "earth crusher". The class was making fun of my shoes because I had on tie up Buster Brown shoes. They were trying to bully me. But what those classmates didn't know was I had on the best shoes money could buy at that time. (I hadn't got my buckle up ones yet.) My classmates would also find other ways to make fun of me and they called me bird lips and bubble-eyed green frog. I never told anyone because I knew that once I got home to all my family and friends the mean things said to me at school didn't matter. Nevertheless, that bullying left me with a scar and is one of the reasons I started standing up for the underdog. I am still that way today. I want to be everybody's savior.

Sister Bike Rides

It's early afternoon on Saturday, all chores are done. I hollered "Come on it's time to go ride our bikes!" All of my sisters yelled, "Ok let's go!" Our bike rides were always fun. It was a must that we rode fast and stood up while riding so we could peddle like champions. The four of us all had different color bikes. Mine was red and blue. Back then, we had baskets on the front of the handles to carry whatever we might need along the way. We never really went too far, Momma and Daddy wouldn't allow it.

On this particular day, let me tell you, I was pumping those peddles, trying to be Miss Fancy. I could feel the breeze in my hair, I mean I was having a ball! I didn't have a care in the world. At one point I turned around and yelled "Come on slow pokes, what's taking you so long?" All of a sudden, I lost my balance and went tumbling down to the ground. My sisters came running as fast as they could asking, "Nialah are you ok?" I was crying so hard; my knee was bleeding and it hurt really badly. That long walk home seemed to take hours. As we approached the house my sisters ran quickly in the house to tell Momma what had happened. She came running to my rescue asking if I was ok. She quickly went and got all that was needed to patch me up.

After she dressed my knee, she leaned over and kissed my knee, and asked did that make it feel better? I smiled and said yes. Now this scar, that is left on my knee still til this day, is such a sweet scar because Momma was there to make me feel good with her kiss of love.

Saturday Morning Ironing Time

The refrigerator was our guide for weekly and daily chores. Nobody ever had to ask what day we were supposed to do which chore, it was all written out for us on a piece of paper that was placed on the refrigerator. We never had to argue or fight because our mother made sure we knew what was expected from each one of us. That list made our lives so much easier. Did we always want to do what was assigned? Of course not. One thing for sure was after all the chores were complete, we had the rest of the day to have fun.

On one particular day it was my time to iron. Someone else had to take the clothes off the line and put them in the clothes basket for me to iron. That day, and on most iron days, I had a pile of clothes that seemed to reach the sky. After a while I had ironed so many clothes that I was exhausted, so I decided to let the ironing board down a little, to try to ease the strain on my body. I didn't realize that I was lowering it too low. While ironing, the iron swiped my thigh. I mean that iron burned me pretty badly. Momma scolded me while she was dressing my burn. She also gently comforted me. That scar is still on my leg today. This scar reminds me to pay close attention to what I'm doing and to obey my parents.

Divorce

Divorce comes in many shapes and sizes, no two are the same. When my parents divorced, it truly was painful. We were a very tight-knit family, I thought. The most painful part for me was the sibling separation that was ordered by the court system. We all were scared. The scar of this divorce and separation turned into rebellion and that rebellion caused me to reject authority.

A lot of things happened during the divorce, and I believe we all were drawn a lot closer to God. We were taught to get on our knees every night and pray before bed. Our prayers touched heaven's gate for sure and after ten years of divorce our parents reunited. They lived happily ever after until my dad passed at age 80. Our scars had been healed and today we remain an extremely tight-knit family. For us, being together is a must.

Abuse

As a teenager I was abused by an adult who was also my so-called "boyfriend". I don't know which hurt worse, the sexual abuse or the physical abuse. The physical abuse hurt because, as a teenager, I thought I was so in love. My boyfriend was three or four years older than me, and he became a terrorizer. He would consistently beat me to a pulp, and the scars left on my body made me feel like I was the ugliest woman in the world. The negative words spoken to me scarred me for a long time. I was and still am so grateful to God for delivering me and my family from him. Today when I look in the mirror I see beauty, but it took many years for me to get to that point. (Read my book "Free at Last".)

Triumphant

Today all I have is Joy, Joy, Joy, down deep in my soul. I took all my scars and turned them into amazing marks of grace. Today I am a Master Spiritual Esthetician, and my life is full of joy.

I encourage you, as I have encouraged others, to not be afraid to recreate yourself. Don't take your scars and hide them in a box somewhere and don't close the book on your life. As long as there is breath in your body you have the opportunity to write the rest of your story. Nobody ever said life would be a breeze. I hope you understand that there is healing for our past wounds and scars. I pray healing for any wounds or scars you've been carrying, whether big or small. Allow the loving Father God to heal you of all your present and past scars. Please allow him to comfort you in places you hurt. Let Him draw you nearer, to receive the gift of healing.

In my past I have had Spirit, Soul and Body scars. I am a spirit, I have a soul, and I live in a body. I began to teach my spirit by listening to great inspirational words about me, and my spirit has healed. My soul was tore up from the floor up and I had to learn to control my emotions. I could no longer constantly beat myself up about my past. I got counseling, which is one of the best things I could have done. Therapy, if needed, is a must. Our emotions can continue to lead us down a road of destruction if we don't get help.

Reaching out to help others was one of the other things that helped me turn my life around. I became a counselor at my church and had the opportunity to mentor many women. It was so satisfying, and I did this for over 20 years. I began to take battered women into my home to teach them how to be strong. So many of the women's stories were worse than mine. Helping them helped to heal me.

The physical abuse I endured left me with an incredibly low amount of self-esteem. I thought I was so ugly. My abuser consistently blacked my eyes. He broke my nose and once hurt my leg so badly that it was close to needing amputation. I was a wreck when it came to my appearance. Thankfully, the women at my church helped me to think better of my appearance. They changed my life because they always told me I was beautiful. Over and over and over again, they would say you are so pretty or you're so beautiful. I finally began to look myself in the mirror and say "Nialah, you don't look so bad after all."

It was around this time that I decided I wanted to become a make-up artist. It was one of the best decisions I could have made. I became a Beauti-Control Consultant, which allowed me to not only beautify my clients' outward appearances, but also help them uncover the beauty of their characters. I think I worked at every make-up counter in my local mall, and I was surprised to learn how many women were ashamed of how they looked. Several women told me their husbands had never seen them without make-up. That's how ashamed they were.

As a Beauti-Control Consultant I was not licensed to touch my client's skin, and that was a problem for me. So I decided to go to college to become a Licensed Esthetician, specializing in skin and body care. I was so happy to be able to assist women with their acne scars, hyperpigmentation, and so many other skin and body problems. You talk about rewarding! I taught my clients not to hide their faces with make-up; make-up is only to enhance. I had many clients who hated their skin tone, they thought they were "too dark". They had been scarred all their lives by stereotypes suggesting that their skin tone wasn't beautiful. Being able to help them get a little glow to their complexion changed their lives, and mine, forever.

Eventually, I decided to open a Day Spa so that I could really pour into

25

women. Every day I had the opportunity to minister to the spirit, soul, and body of each of my clients. Women would come in with all kinds of stories. My Day Spa was a place for women to come for professional care and for peace. Having peace is the ultimate survival tool one needs to flourish when healing from life's scars.

The most rewarding part of my journey was becoming a Therapeutic Counselor for the State of North Carolina. For over ten years I worked in group homes and counseled teenagers who were dealing with a variety of different issues. Being a rebellious teenager myself, I had all the tools needed to help them become better citizens and to have a positive influence in their communities.

I can say that God is good, He made a way for me. He turned my life around. He placed my feet on solid ground. I get Joy when I think about what He has done for me. I am happily married to a wonderful, kind man. I have four beautiful children and three grandchildren. I am an author of a few books, I am a speaker, teacher, a certified wellness consultant. I speak twice a week on WPGR radio broadcast and on TV. I also received a Doctorate from Breakthrough Bible College. Over the years I have received so many certificates, awards and honorees for the work I have done in my life. All I can say is Thank You Father for being so good to me. For I am Prophetess Dr. Nialah Ali.

* * *

What the scriptures reveal about scars:

- Proverbs 27:6 Faithful are the wounds of a friend, But deceitful are the kisses of an enemy.

- Zechariah 13:6 And one will say to him, "What are these wounds between your arms?" Then he will say, "Those with which I was wounded in the house of my friends."

- Proverbs 23:29 Who has woe? Who has sorrow? Who has contentions? Who has complaining? Who has wounds without cause?

- Jeremiah 30:17 "For I will restore you to health and I will heal you of your wounds," declares the Lord, "because they have called you an outcast, saying: "It is Zion no one cares for her."

- Psalms 147:3 He heals the brokenhearted, and binds up their wounds.

HE Was There All The Time

Gary C. Bass

HE Was There All The Time

Gary C. Bass

I was born in Harlem, NY in the early 1950s. Back then Harlem was not a good place to live.

I had an aunt who worked for GE and lived in East Orange, NJ. My mother sent me to live with her at an early age. I lived with her until I was six years old and about to start school. My aunt contacted my mother to get my birth certificate so she could register me for school. My mom told my aunt she wanted me to come back to New York, so I was sent back to Harlem to live.

My mom was my rock and my best friend. She taught me how to do things for myself, such as how to wash clothes, iron, and do a limited amount of cooking. I attended Catholic church and was an altar boy in church.

Then suddenly my world came down and crashed on me. I was eleven years old, and my mom passed away from pneumonia! I vividly remember someone knocking on the door to tell my stepdad that my mom had died. I couldn't understand why God took my mom away from me. After all, I went to church and I also served Him.

Well, at that point, I fell out with God and didn't want anything to do with Him.

My stepdad didn't want to take care of me and my youngest sister, so my grandmother who lived in Union, NJ took us. One of my chores there was to wash dishes from time to time.

On one particular day, I didn't want to wash dishes, so I went into a bowl of pennies my grandmother had on top of the china cabinet. From this bowl I grabbed a handful of pennies (11 to be exact) and offered them to my cousin who had come over. I told her that she could have the 11 pennies if she'd wash the dishes for me. She agreed and rested the pennies on the windowsill. When my grandmother came home, she asked my cousin where she got the money. My cousin told her she got them from me. When my grandmother asked me where I got them, I told her I had gone to the store to buy candy and got the pennies as change. Of course, she knew a lie when she heard one. She proceeded to beat my butt and called my biological dad to tell him I was a liar and a thief, and she was bringing me back to NY to live with him. Back to New York I went!

Living in Harlem in the 60's was tough to say the least. Drugs were everywhere. I had a sister die from AIDS she contracted from a hypodermic needle. There were gangs and muggings, and robberies took place all the time. It was like living in a war zone. I don't know how I survived, but I did.

While in Junior High School the aunt that I lived with until my mom wanted me back came to New York and asked my dad if I could live with her again. While living with her, one of my chores was to put coal in the furnace and keep the fire going. One night I heard her talking to her friend and she said "he puts the coal in the furnace, but he doesn't sweep up the coals that fall to the floor. I can't take this so I'm sending him back to New York." So back to New York I went!

I lived in a rooming house and had a room big enough for a single bed and a dresser. I had to go into the hall to use the bathroom. My dad's room was at the opposite end of the hall, so I rarely saw him. I would go to school, go home, do my homework, and then go to the night center where I could play basketball, pool, ping pong, and listen to music.

While in high school, I was offered a part time job with IBM. I was chosen by my guidance counselor because I got a 99 on the NY State Regents exam in Algebra. Soon after, I was offered a scholarship to attend City College of New York. In the meantime, my manager at IBM offered me a full-time job and suggested that I go to college at night. By this time I was used to having a few coins in my pocket, so I accepted the job and enrolled at Rutgers University to take classes at night.

I progressed at IBM and was transferred to numerous positions in New Jersey, Maryland, Florida, Boston, and then back to Maryland.

In 1990 I was dating a woman who said that if I wanted to be with her, I had to go to church. Although I was still angry with God, I agreed to go. It was during one of those church services that I felt as if the Pastor was preaching directly to me. And I started thinking about how God had sent His angels to protect me from the drugs, gangs, and unsafe environment of my youth. How God had provided me an opportunity to get a job at IBM and to get several promotions. How He had blessed me with two beautiful daughters. What a joy it was to realize that He was there all the time!

I praise God each day. I give Him praise for His goodness and mercy. I thank Him for being Jehovah Jireh and providing all my needs. For making a way when there seemed to be no way. And for gracing me with His remarkable, unspeakable joy. He was there all the time and continues to be there.

That Little Bundle of Joy

Gail Clanton

That Little Bundle of Joy

Gail Clanton

It didn't start out well, this relationship we have. You see, before we'd even met, I had pretty much decided that I didn't like him. I didn't need him. I was fine being the only child.

Nonetheless, against my wishes, he came home one cool October day. I can vaguely remember the first time I saw him, even though I was only four years old. His eyes, ears, and nose were in the proper places, and though I didn't want to admit it, he was actually kinda cute.

Even so, I remember being disappointed that he didn't do more than just eat and sleep. I shared this concern with my parents, and it was a joke in future years. But, when I was four, it wasn't funny. All that baby did was eat and sleep! Cute or not, I expected more. As I saw it at the time, if I HAD to have a baby brother, at least he could be fun! Why did I have a brother who didn't do anything? To me, it seemed grossly unfair.

As time progressed, I began see more in him, he showed potential, and he seemed ok. Sometimes he even managed to be fun. Until he got teeth.

Do you remember the records we called 45s? Do you remember when they were in different colors? I had a yellow one and it played "Wake Me Shake Me, Don't Let Me Sleep Too Late" and that's the first record my baby brother chose to bite into and crack with his teeth. Shortly thereafter he broke my second favorite record, "I Wanna Hold

Your Hand" by the Beatles. I was a little Black girl living in Washington, DC, I really don't know why I had such a thing for that song, but I did, and I loved that record as much as life itself.

As time went on, he stopped cracking records and began to develop a gentler personality, and I sometimes enjoyed this little boy. By now I'd grown to realize that he wasn't going away and I began calling him "Brother", a nickname that we continue to use when addressing him.

We shared the same vivid imagination and would make up stories involving our imaginary friends, including ZimaZoom and her mom, whom we simply referred to as "ZimaZoom's Mother". Then there was also Man, Boy, Otis, and a host of other characters. We also shared a love of music and movies. Speaking of movies...

There was the time I wanted so badly to go to the movies with my friends and my mother said that I could only go if I took my brother. If you're an older sibling, perhaps you can relate. On that day I took my brother, but I didn't like it. But, excuse me, I digress.

The point I was starting to make is that after a while I began to see value in my little brother and that value intensified as the years progressed.

By our teen years we were friends. Well, sorta. I guess we were half-way friends. I mean, we were the kind of friends who rolled their eyes at each other often and called each other names on a regular basis. We were the kind of friends who would beat you down if you committed an egregious "crime" like eating the last of the ice cream or lingering in the bathroom for too long on any given morning, or for not staying completely on your side of back seat of our parents' car. You know, serious matters like that. And did we fight!

Our battles left us both bruised, emotionally, and physically. Even so, this was my little brother and I'd fight you if you bothered him. I could hit him, but you certainly could not.

As the years went on, I began to value our relationship even more fully. And now, as a full-grown adult and borderline senior citizen, I love him with every ounce of my being. My relationship with him brings me pure, complete, overwhelming, unabbreviated, cup-runneth-over, JOY.

My brother has been with me through the happiest and most difficult moments of my life. He's like an unexpected ray of sunshine or a summer breeze that shows up just when you least expect it, but when you need it most.

When our father passed away, my brother silently and without much pomp or circumstance, accepted his role as the patriarch of our family. That torch has passed, and we have all benefitted from his presence. My father would be so incredibly proud of him.

And, while going through the dark days of my divorce, I counted on my brother for wise counsel, comic relief, and overall support. I will never forget seeing him at the door of my ex-husband's house the morning I was packing to leave. I didn't know he was coming, but there he was, just the ray of sunshine I needed. I didn't know I needed him until he was there. His presence made everything better.

Then there were the countless court appearances that I never had to deal with on my own. Like clockwork, my brother was always there. His quiet confidence (inherited from our father) and his practical, no-nonsense wisdom (inherited from our mother) made every moment I spent at the courthouse easier to bear.

Now, as a single woman, my brother looks out for me in more ways than I can count. I don't have to worry about anything because I know that my brother is just a phone call away. He helps me sort through challenging situations, maneuver life's odd moments, and helps me plot my next moves. And let me not forget to mention the home repairs he so graciously does for me.

We find humor in the same ridiculous things and share jokes that I don't think anyone else on the planet would understand. In a nutshell, I don't know what I'd do without this little brother whom I didn't think I wanted in my life. Not only do I WANT him in my life, I NEED him in my life and I hope he'll forgive me for the times that I behaved as if I didn't.

In his presence I feel joy. In his presence I AM joy. And I'm forced to ask the question, "Whose life is better because of the joy I bring? And what's the big deal about joy anyway?"

I appreciate the concept of joy because it describes a feeling that is internal. You can feel joy in the midst of a storm, because joy isn't reactionary. It isn't dictated by the environment. Like the song states, the world didn't give us joy and the world can't take it away. Joy is an inside job.

For me this means that within me at all times is the capacity to be joyous and to share joy with others. There's always someone who needs my joy and sometimes that "someone" may be me.

Joy encourages, joy loves, joy supports, joy laughs. It helps and it heals.

Joy shows up in unexpected packages. It may not look or sound like you think it should, but that doesn't dim its sparkle or compromise its power.

The Bible states that the joy of the Lord is my strength. I'm blessed to be able to couple that joy with the love and sense of security I feel from that little bundle of joy I met one October afternoon. I am fully convinced that God gave me the brother I have because of the joy He knew I'd need and enjoy.

I thank God for my brother and for the joy he brings to so many people… not the least of whom is me.

> *"If you keep my commandments, you will abide in my love, just as I have kept my Father's commandments and abide in his love. These things I have spoken to you, that my joy may be in you, and that your joy may be full. 'This is my commandment, that you love one another as I have loved you.'" - John 15:10–12*

That Elusive Thing Called Joy

George D. Clanton

That Elusive Thing Called Joy

George D. Clanton

The simple fact that a book like this needed to be written supports the notion that "Joy" is difficult to come by. Prior to the pandemic, church houses were filled each week with folks looking for it in the scriptures, in the preaching, in the praying, in the music, and even in one another! And we can agree that there are lots of books, TV shows, and podcasts all designed to bring happiness, laughter, and joy. But, what is joy and is it really that hard to find? I would argue that if we remove the "scales from our eyes", we will discover joy right in front of us. Just as the clear blue sky is always there even on the cloudiest of days; likewise, joy is ever present.

Like many people of a certain age, I have recently been thinking a lot about my life and my legacy. I graduated from college decades ago. I am on the tail end of my career. My lovely wife and I have raised three wonderful children. So, I wonder. Who am I? What is my purpose? Have my activities, my focus, my accomplishments supported GOD's purpose for my life? Do I feel any sense of fulfilment? Sure, I have "things". I have a home and a car. I have been on nice vacations. But, I often feel a disconnect between the work I do and my purpose. I work in the IT field overseeing large government contracts for the procurement of computer software. Somehow, as GOD sat on high contemplating my creation, I don't think this is quite the contribution to His kingdom here on earth that He had in mind for me.

At one point, I thought I should be a teacher. My parents were both teachers. Teachers are awesome. They make important contributions to society, to their communities, to the world. That's it, I thought – I should teach! So, I arranged to get an interview for a teaching position at my old high school. At the time, it had not been that long since I graduated; so, many of the faculty and staff I knew were still there. In fact, my Biology teacher (one of my favorites) was now the Principal! I was sure I had it made. The interview went well; but it didn't work out. I had the zeal, but lacked the credentials.

At one point, I thought I should be a lawyer. Lawyers help people out. They advocate for those who need help navigating the legal system. I would open a small office and folks would come to me with their problems and I would help them. What could be more noble than that?

So, I reached out to several local law schools and found a very helpful person at the University of the District of Columbia Law School who very nicely explained to me that they did not have a part-time program. It didn't work out because I was not in a financial position to quit my job and pursue legal studies on a full-time basis.

At one point, I thought I should go to seminary. Of course, I thought. This is it! No more fooling around. If I wanted my vocation to make a contribution to the world and be in line with GOD's purpose for my life, then learn how to minister! I discovered there are multiple career paths for seminarians. It's not just for folks wanting to be pastors. I looked over the various programs and decided I would study Pastoral Counseling. I would be something like a therapist, but from a Christian perspective. My father had spent some of his career as a school counselor; so, this felt right.

The hunt was on for the right school. I attended open houses where students, recent graduates, and faculty spoke about the programs and job opportunities. At one such event, a faculty member gave a brief lecture so the attendees could get a feel for what seminary study would be like. It was so cool to attend a lecture that was like a sermon! It didn't feel like a lecture at all. I had an undergraduate degree; so, there were no issues with my credentials. They had a part-time program; so, I could attend classes while still maintaining my full-time job. I submitted my application and it was good enough to be called in for an interview. The interview went well and I was offered admission! I was so excited. I announced the good news to my wife and kids. My kids joked that, once classes started, they would be asking me about my "homework situation", which is how I always phrased it to them. Well ahead of receiving an actual course schedule, I looked online to find out which textbooks I would need and ordered a few on Amazon. I wanted to immerse myself. I wanted to get a head start.

This all happened in the fall and the semester would start in late January. An online account had been set up for me and I logged in regularly waiting for the tuition bill to show up. It never did. I reached out to the professor with whom I had interviewed and eventually found out that the school was going out of business! They were going to stay in business long enough to graduate those who had already started the program; but, they were not going to be around long enough for me to finish on a part-time basis. So, that was that. I did search for other programs; but, I lost my zeal and just continued my work for the federal government.

For many years and in many ways, I put those thoughts on the back burner. But, now that I have reached that certain age, those thoughts started coming up again. When I reached 50, I discovered my minimum retirement age was 56. In six short years, I thought, I would be able to retire from the government, drawing a modest pension that could be used to augment the salary I would make doing the job of my dreams – the work I was always meant to do, that would bring me that elusive sense of fulfilment and joy, that would make a contribution to the world, that would bring a smile to GOD's face, that would cause Him to say: "he's finally got it!"

Six years came and went, and I still had not figured out my Plan B. And then, it dawned on me. I think the scales fell from my eyes and I was able to see that blue sky that had been there all along. The idea of scales obscuring one's vision is from the story of Saul/Paul. There are two things in that story from Acts 9 that speak to me.

As you recall, Saul took great joy in persecuting Christians – and he was really good at it. On the road to Damascus, a light from heaven appeared that was so intense that he fell off his horse and he cried out (now get this): "Who are you, LORD"? Obviously, he knew who it was because he called the LORD by name! That's like my sister telling me that I was in trouble and my immediate response being: "I don't know anything about any Beatles record!". (Not sure what this means? See Gail Clanton's story.) While Saul had made it his life's mission to destroy anyone who would dare to believe in JESUS, his immediate capitulation to GOD's sovereignty in this situation is very telling. If he believed in his heart what he had been "preaching", it would never have occurred to him to call out to the LORD. So, he knew all along that GOD is real.

The second thing I noticed comes in verse 18 where the Bible records that, after being blinded by that heavenly light for three days, "something like scales fell from Saul's eyes, and he could see again".

His sight was not only restored; it was renewed, and he went out to get himself baptized. After that, he went on to fearlessly preach the Gospel for the rest of his days.

So, how does this relate to my story?

Well, in my own small way, I feel like the scales are falling from my eyes. I feel like blessings and opportunities to be a blessing are all around me and have been all along. I work for a federal agency whose mission includes insuring the health and safety of the American people. Talk about making a contribution to society!

Perhaps, in my IT role, I am not as connected to this as others; but I recognize I am in an ideal position to make that connection. Over the years, I have conducted numerous professional training sessions on various topics. So, maybe I got to be a teacher after all. I am also responsible for bringing different groups together to solve technical problems. As simple as it sounds: one group will have a need and another group will have a solution; but, they need someone to bring them together, to facilitate the discussion, to advocate for what is needed and to assist with the negotiation. So, while I never went to Law School, I have excelled in this type of role and helped my agency be productive in this way time and time again.

In light of the pandemic, my church, like many others, has relied more and more on technology. We use it to bring the services, including the music, to the computer desktops and mobile devices of our congregation members and friends all over the world via the internet. Even though I am not really a musician (more a music enthusiast), I was asked to be the Music Director shortly before the pandemic started. As a result of what is happening in our world, we have needed to pivot from the traditional music ministry – a praise team rendering live music in front of a full room of people singing along – to something altogether different. I have to find accompaniment tracks and work with praise team members individually (no more groups unless they are family members) to record themselves singing the song in a manner that supports social distancing. Sometimes the accompaniment is too long, too short, too slow, too fast, or in the wrong key for the singer. So, I use software to make any needed adjustments.

I have also figured out how to create virtual choir selections where each singer -- soprano, alto, and tenor -- is recorded individually and then all the parts are brought together into a Hollywood Squares-type presentation. I had no prior background in this so I had to learn a lot and it has taken many hours of painstaking trial and error to produce something that looked good enough to present. But it has been a BLAST. I enjoy it so much. It has sparked a creativity I did not know I had. Each video project provides a new opportunity to touch GOD's people in a new way. Last Christmas, I was especially proud of one video that included praise team members singing while a slide show of candid pictures of our members taken from Christmases in the past was playing. The song selection was on point and the pictures allowed us to see faces we had not seen in person for such a long time. It wasn't preaching. It wasn't Pastoral Counseling. But I knew in my heart that this work was making a contribution and I feel that this is right where GOD wants me to be.

So, in the same way, I encourage you to keep your eyes open for the blessings and the opportunities for JOY that are right in front of you. They may not look like you expect them to look. They may not come when you expect them to come. But they are right there waiting for you. My hope is you don't waste a moment searching for what is already within your reach.

I Unmasked H.E.R. To Live Unpretentiously Joyous!

Betsy Evans-Bennett

I Unmasked H.E.R. To Live Unpretentiously Joyous!

Betsy Evans-Bennett

Have you ever wondered why you settled or why you tolerated all the pain, heartache, suffering, and ungratefulness that was issued out to you? Have you ever just had random thoughts about what life would look like or even be like if you chose to put yourself first? Have you ever found yourself wishing, hoping dreaming for change to come? Guess what! I have!

I have wondered and wished and dreamt of so many things, but what I soon realized was that I had to make things happen. If I needed a change I had to be that change. Oftentimes we go through life thinking that someone or something else is responsible for making us happy. Wrong! As individuals we are responsible for our own state of being, and that includes our happiness.

There was a time in my life when my entire being was centered around a man and a marriage and I was blinded to the fact that this was not for me. It was a roller coaster ride to hell through a whirlwind of never-ending anguish and pain, but I believed he was my forever and so to him I relinquished all power. He was in total control. I didn't know my worth, no value was placed on my being, and that accounted for all I was going through. I suffered for years as an abused spouse all because I placed myself on the back row of my own life and gave first class seating to someone else.

What you must understand is that your value isn't found in anyone else, it's not in what you have nor what you do but rather in who you are. Our value comes from the labels we put on ourselves. If we attach a "damaged goods" label then we are valued as such. If we attach a "designer's original" label then you best bet we will be valued as such.

> *"You will be as much value to others as you are to yourself."*
> *- Marcus T Cicero*

I was in hiding. I was masking my true worth, my potential, my abilities, my gifts, my talents, and my skills. I wasn't in pursuit of my dreams nor anything that made me happy and set my soul on fire. I masked my pain with a pretentious smile. I appeared to everyone as the happy-go-lucky girl, but I was silently dying inside. Yes, I was the great pretender. I had given up on my goals and dreams to facilitate a life with a man. I had lost the true essence of being me and what resulted was me merely existing and not living.

Was this the life that God had ordained? At what point would I redesign my own life? What would it take for me to put myself first? Not in a selfish way, but that I would first overdose myself with love and allow others to feast from my overflow.

The worst part about all this was that I was brought up on Bible truths, and the upkeep of my charade was not God-ordained. This wasn't my life and it sure wasn't my destiny. Jeremiah 29:11 clearly states the Almighty's intentions towards me: "For I know the plans I have for you declares the Lord; plans to prosper you and not to harm you, plans to give you hope and a future." Where in this Scripture did it say God's plans for me was humiliation, pain, anger, frustration, and shame? This period was undoubtedly the roughest part of my life up to this point. Through it all I never gave up, I never gave in, I had that hope that I would someday walk in my true calling and live out my purpose.

I am and have always been a dreamer and this gave me that glimpse of hope that light was coming up at the end of the tunnel. As a prayer warrior, yes I prayed and patiently waited for manifestations, but I also had to master the concept that "it all begins with me." I had to make the first step. God promised to lead me through the tides of life, but He will not make the journey for me. I had to "faith up" and courageously start trusting God through the process. Who said it was going to be easy? I can tell you it wasn't, but I had to find the strength to snatch my power back and regain control. This was my life and I was going to do it my way!

Allan Rufus said "Life is like a game of chess. To win you have to make a move. Knowing which move to make comes with insight and knowledge, and by learning the lessons that are accumulated along the way. We become each and every piece within the game called life."

As I entered a new season of my life, I was reminded that there is a time and a place for everything under the sun. I used this thought as I revved up my engine to propel myself into my next, with freedom and happiness as my ultimate goals. Without any hesitations I started preparing to exit a season that was never mine to begin with. I was demitting the office of abuse, pain, shame, fear, frustration, anger, sadness, betrayal, and unhappiness to assume my new leadership role in the prestigious capacity of self-love, self-care, self-appreciation, self-worth, self-respect, and self-confidence. This was my season of new beginnings, and I was going to show up! Yes, my nerves racked and fear gripped me at times, but I found strength through reaffirmation each day. I AM ENOUGH, I AM WORTHY, I AM CHOSEN, I AM

A WARRIOR, I AM CONFIDENT, I AM STRONG,

I AM ABLE THROUGH JESUS CHRIST MY LORD! Philippians 4:13 "I can do all things through Christ who strengthens me."

It was now time for the butterfly concept to take full effect. Did you know that the butterfly didn't have a beautiful beginning? Oh no! It was all a process. This is referred to as metamorphosis.

- **1st:** The egg; the conception process; this is where the thought is conceived.

- **2nd:** The larva; this stage is the caterpillar stage; it is the feeding or nourishing stage, hence this is where you nurture your thoughts or ideas conceived in stage 1. Whatever you nourish will grow.

- **3rd:** The pupa; this is the chrysalis; it is the transition stage. Rapid growth and expansion take place here. Development, everything you thought of nourished and nurtured is now coming together in preparation for birthing.

- **4th:** The adult; this is now that beautiful butterfly; it is the reproductive stage. This is where you begin to show up. This is where the beautiful butterfly engages its wings and takes flight.

My dear hearts, life is a cycle just as that of a butterfly. It rarely starts out beautiful or already made but through transition the end can be amazing! I went through my metamorphosis, and you can too! I was radically changed from a caterpillar to a beautiful butterfly. Yes!

1. I made the conscious decision to leave that abusive season.

2. I processed and gave much thought to how I should proceed.

3. I sought help as to the steps I needed to take in order to effectively make my exit.

4. Now I'm out! Praise God, I am ready to soar!

I knew this was it for me. No more holding back, no more denying me, I was now in my own lane and undoubtedly in charge of maintenance. I now owned ME. All rights sustained. Bit by bit I started to embrace my truth, to love on me, to reboot my confidence. I had stepped fully into my world and unapologetically owned it. This was a clean slate and I had the honor, privilege, and the audacity of designing it my own way with help from Almighty God. He had given me another chance at life, and I was going to color it beautiful.

I don't know where you are in your metamorphosis at this point in your life but believe me when I tell you as that butterfly cracks open and breaks free from its cocoon, so too can you break free from whatever has you bounded. I had now unmasked the pretentious H.E.R and was truly living in the key of joy. My happiness had taken flight and I was soaring on its wings. The view from above was amazingly beautiful.

My mission is now to show up for others and aid them in their own transformation wherever they are in their own metamorphosis. We all should remember the words of Oprah Winfrey: "Your life isn't about a big break. It's about one significant life transforming step at a time."

Today I am well on my way to becoming the woman my daughter can truly respect and admire. My resilience, bravery, determination to win, and my unwavering faith in God has taken me thus far and God is still not through with me yet. Right here, right now, I am free. I have emerged. In breaking free I proved that I was no longer a pawn being pushed and pulled, but a powerful queen. I stand ready to accept and exercise my rights in my royal position. At this point Queen Esther has nothing on me! What an amazing feeling!

I learned very fast that in life we have three choices: give up, give in, or give it all you've got. I chose the latter. I gave it all I had. Life is a journey, but our trajectory is up to us. We are in charge of paving our own path. When love and trust fail, it takes courage, guts, and your faith in God to withstand. Through the failures the fact remains "life goes on." My marriage failed; life goes on. I got a divorce; life goes on. I became single and a single mom; heck…guess what! Life goes on! It's now a chain reaction. Pain to purpose aligned with destiny. I am boldly walking in my calling, now living my God-ordained life. Self-discovery and transformation brought on beauty that didn't exist before, "the beauty of life." This was one of the most profound and breathtaking moments of my life. I am waking up now wanting to be me. Not wishing I was someone else. I wake up every morning choosing to be me. Yes me! How beautiful is that? Choosing with every breaking of dawn to be ME. This happiness is enriching.

I'm so glad that I took the risk. I did the work. My wings didn't just grow overnight and the accolades weren't just awarded. It took strength, dedication, determination, commitment, and drive. My mother always told me "no matter how the winds gust and the tides rise, a strong soul will shine after every storm." I dared to be bold, I dared to be true, I dared to be different, I dared to be ME.

This all had a "suddenly" attached to it. Suddenly life had new meaning. Suddenly life became a blessing, Suddenly I just started living. My blessing was wrapped up in saying good-bye to the old and welcoming the new. The experience that fueled my motivation to live a life of pure joy, I would not wish on my worst enemy, but I'm grateful that God gave me strength to endure. I am humbled to have crossed my Jordan and I ain't going back.

My best inspiration in the quest of a better life, was my daughter. Her look of innocence I dared not toy with. Her bright sunlit smile I couldn't imagine turning to sadness or a frown. I had to protect her space, her peace. Her happiness relied on my own. Selfishness wasn't an option. We are a true reflection of decisions made. Accountability always follows. I am in a better place all because of the choices I made. I am no longer a slave of fear. I am now confidently living my dreams all because I chose to:

1. **SHED-** I left behind what wasn't for me. I detached myself from all unhealthy entanglements and acquaintances. I broke up with every ounce of negativity. I ditched fear (fear is the thief of all joy) and engaged faith.

2. **SHIFT-** I got out of neutral and kicked off in full gear. I accepted the "now" with a renewed mindset. I embraced the new ME with all hope and possibilities, believing my best was still yet to come.

3. **SHOW UP-** I enhanced the beauty of new life, new beginnings. I radiated the true essence of self. I unapologetically answered purpose and am brilliantly striding in my calling. I am making waves by using my talent, abilities, gifts, and skills to light the way for others to walk in their truth and be their own kind of beautiful.

After all this, I can now say:

Dear ME,

I am so sorry for all that I have allowed to cause you pain. For all the bad decisions I made. For all the wrong turns I took that drove you through hell and back. For not realizing your value and worth, and for compromising one of the most important aspects of your life, your happiness. What an adventure this has been in your voyage for harmony, peace, love, and joy. Life has proven true in being a marathon and not a sprint. I am grateful you endured and withstood the tests of time.

You never gave up, though you fell, cried, crashed and burned. You fought relentlessly in your pursuit of happiness and this shew forth true strength, bravery, vigor, confidence, consistency, optimism, and resilience. You aren't just the epitome of pure beauty but also of a true queen. You represent well a modern-day Esther. I am peacock proud of your exponential growth with compound interest and your versatile ability to live life with little or no regrets. Like a champion, you accepted your mistakes and challenges as part of a learning process instead of allowing them to become reasons to wallow in a pity party.

You, Betsy, are authentically a masterpiece. You have proven to yourself and others that if you can dream it you can attain it. You've classified yourself a dreamer, so keep on dreaming my darling, your story is still being written, your best is still yet to come. Until then just know I'm super proud of the woman you are becoming, and always remember no matter what lies ahead of you, God is already there. My prayer is that you will continue designing the life you love and graciously bask in every moment of it.

Xoxo Betsy.
H.E.R. (Hero Evolving Relentlessly)

A Labor of Love

Yolanda Fields-Witherspoon

A Labor of Love

Yolanda Fields-Witherspoon

During my teens and young adulthood, I never thought that my parents would get "old" or as I like to say, "become more seasoned in life." However, fast forward to the present and I, as well as my parents, have become more "seasoned". I must say that the very thought of it all is very humbling.

The Word of God states, "Honor your father and your mother, as the Lord your God has commanded you." (Deuteronomy 5:16 NKJV). I learned this Scripture during childhood, and it has been engrafted in my heart ever since. Now, as an adult, this Scripture is helping me to endure the challenges I face as I care for my parents.

The Word of God also states in I Corinthians 13:4,7 & 8, "Love suffers long and is kind: 7 bears all things, believes all things, hopes all things, endures all things. 8 Love never fails". (NKJV). I never realized the depth and power of true love until I've had to help take care of the person who birthed me and nurtured me to become the person I am today. Although painful at times to see my parents changing before my eyes, the deep love I have for them is what helps me to keep standing even in the midst of adversity.

Honor and love are two words that have taken on a deeper meaning in my life as now that I have the opportunity to pour into my parents' lives as they have so graciously, lovingly and unconditionally poured into mine. Their care for me has made me the person I am today. I know I can never duplicate their many labors of love, but I put forth a huge effort every day to do just that.

Throughout my life, my parents have been an inspiration to me, as they have always had a heart to serve their loved ones. They have traveled the extra mile to secure clothing, food, and shelter for individuals and their reach has extended both near and far. My parents always shared vegetables and fruits from their abundant summer gardens and were even once highlighted on a local news show because of their many acts of kindness. They also participated in feeding the homeless and prepared meals for the homebound.

They never once complained or tried to take the shortcut, rather they always unselfishly gave of their time as they rose to meet the need of the person they were called to help. They served from their hearts and they did so with great joy and honor. They taught my siblings and me to do the same.

Prior to December 2019, my mother was always on the go, preparing meals, ministering to the sick, and delivering groceries to family and friends in need. She constantly put others first, even before taking care of her own needs, and she always did so with excitement and joy. She exuded so much excitement that I often volunteered to help her as she helped others.

That excitement spilled over into her entrepreneurship as the first Black Tupperware Manager and top seller in the Richmond, Virginia area. Seeing my mother operating in her gift of service was such a blessing to me.

My mother was also always the designated driver when traveling on day and weekend trips with her friends and family members. Those trips included Sunday rides on the Ferry, to the mountains, and to

Washington, DC. In addition, she often traveled with me to business conventions. Family vacations were not just for blood relatives, but my parents encouraged friends to travel with us as well. Our annual trip to Orlando, Florida for the Tupperware Convention was always a hit.

My mother loved to shop, cook, sing, read the Word of God, and pray. She also enjoyed spending time with her family and friends, especially her grandchildren and great-grandchildren. She often told me of how she had prayed and asked the Lord to allow her to see her children, grandchildren, and great-grandchildren grow up because her mother passed away at the age of 32 years old.

In December of 2019, things changed in an instant when my nieces called me on that Saturday evening indicating that my mother exhibited difficulty recalling places, following directions, differentiating time and dates, as well as difficulty with her overall balance. She was immediately taken to the emergency room and admitted into the hospital, as her symptoms were deemed to be life-threatening. My mother struggled to remember the year and she couldn't recall the names of all of her children. She struggled with simple tasks, such as putting on her shoes or figuring out how to get around an obstacle in her path. She required intensive inpatient rehabilitation for a month to relearn basic living skills.

Soon I began to notice that my mother was not the same vibrant person who was once so full of energy and life. She was no longer the person I had witnessed my entire life. It appeared as though parts of my mom were fading. She did exhibit ups and downs throughout her hospital stay and time in rehab, but through it all she was determined to accomplish one goal in particular: "return to her home." Thanks be to God; my mother eventually met her goal.

Once Mom became acclimated to being back at home, I noticed some return of that spark that seemed to be lost when she was hospitalized. She engaged in conversation with family and friends, although it was often brief with minimal content. Her best friend offered to sit with her a couple of times per week when we all had to return to work. She appeared to enjoy the time spent with her dear friend but even this "sister" friend noticed that she was not the same. This woman who was once the spark of the family was becoming quiet, and sometimes somewhat withdrawn, right before our very eyes. Seeing this was painful, and this was a time of adjustment for my mother and family. Nevertheless, we made the best of each moment and I focused on the brightness of my mom's smile.

Then, eight months after my mom was discharged from the hospital, we were notified that her best friend, her "sister" friend she could always count on had suddenly passed away. Fortunately, my mother had just talked to her the day before and she was able to tell her how much she loved and missed her, as her best friend had moved. The news of this passing was a pivotal point in my mother's life. Over time I noticed an increased level of sadness with occasional questions regarding her lifetime friend. I also noticed a slight decrease in her ability to recall recent events and day-to-day tasks.

At this time, my sister and I devised a plan for me to visit daily to help make sure our mother's needs were addressed. Although my mother appeared to be reserved at times, in many ways she remained "sharp as a tack", and no one could say anything without her correcting them or interjecting her own views or comments. Those were the times we all would fall out in tears full of laughter.

As 2021 progressed, Mom continued to exhibit memory challenges, and we saw a change in her mood and in her level of activity. She seldom wanted to participate in daily activities, preferring to sit in her favorite chair pretty much the entire day. She would engage in conversation at times; however, the conversation would be brief. Nonetheless, she continued to be very witty and I still couldn't put anything past her. For example, I would call her and ask, "What are you doing?" and her quick response would be, "Talking to you." Or if I asked, "How are you feeling?", her response would be "With my fingers." Of course, both of us would burst into laughter. When I would stop in on my daily visits she would often say, "Gail, I really appreciate everything you do for me. You are a good daughter." Just hearing her say that meant the world to me, and it still does. Through it all she has always maintained a loving, caring, and thoughtful demeanor and being able to serve her is a joy I deeply cherish.

In September of 2021, my mother lost her only brother, which again chipped away another small piece of her. Even now she will ask about him, and there are other times when she asks if he has passed away.

In October of 2021, I had surgery on my shoulder which resulted in me being on sick leave for an extended period of time. Once I was mobile, I stayed with my mother during the day. Now I could really spend quality time with her and attempt to engage her in tasks to facilitate participation and increased brain stimulation. One day I was able to convince her to play a game of Tic-Tac-Toe which resulted in us playing a total of seven games, five of which my mom won. I must say that I did not "allow" her to win; she won those games on her own. The joy I felt to see her face radiate and to hear her boasting about her winnings was worth billions!! Other times we would listen to old hymns. The lyrics of those inspiring, faith-filled songs fluently rolled out of her mouth, and that was true music to my ears. I especially loved hearing her sing her favorite song, "We Shall Behold Him" by Sandy Patty. Oh, what joy filled my heart!

When she was a child, my mother had to care for her own mother when she became gravely ill. Mom has told me stories of how she sometimes wouldn't have food or would have to skip lunch in order to be able to pay for her mother's medication. Now that she's on the receiving end, and receiving all sorts of gifts from others, if she is gifted with something to eat, she is ready to receive it with great appreciation and thanksgiving. Typically, she is not picky, however she can sometimes be resistive and a little challenging to work with when she is not able to choose a favorite dish and/or she wants a snack that is not in her "healthy" choice category. She will eventually comply after several minutes of negotiation. One thing is for sure, we do not have to convince her to eat because she loves to eat and as a matter of fact, she's stated that she is not like most people her age because she has a good appetite.

One morning, I entered her room and she was still in bed and I told her that her breakfast was ready and her response was, "You cooked breakfast for me!!" Another time I asked her, "How are you, Mama?" Her response was, "I'm better since I see you. I love you, Gail, and I thank God for you."

Most days she prefers to stay at home, but my mom does love to ride around once I can get her out of the house. However, just trying to get her out can be a major job. I have to plan for several hours of preparation to allow ample time for us to get to her appointments on time. During our preparation time, she frequently asks me where we're going and why we're going there. This has been painful because she was a person who always kept an appointment book, was organized, memorized information, and loved to travel. However, once we are out and about for the various appointments, she looks forward to going to one of her favorite restaurants afterwards, and getting her favorite entrée, fish.

Although it has been extremely difficult to see the changes that have occurred over the last two years concerning my mother's health (and there have been days I've silently shed tears), I've found that it's more important to choose my battles and to enjoy and cherish the simplest moments of the one's you love. And I've learned to not take anything for granted. As Dr. Cindy Trimm would say, "Live, learn, love, serve and then leave a legacy". So, I'm learning to do just that and laughing and loving hard in the process. I wrote a tribute to my mother prior to the change of events which occurred in December of 2019 and it is as follows:

"Day to day I see you working, teaching, loving, caring for your family with a labor of love. Day to day I see you laughing, smiling, and demonstrating what a mother's love is all about. Day to day I see you doing what is necessary to make it all flow in your home. Day to day I see you being the phenomenal mother you are. I celebrate you for being who you are: An Extra Special Pearl of Great Price!!!"

Caring for Mom has been, and continues to be, a true labor of love, for not only me but for my whole family and our community. It is an honor to serve my mother and I am so grateful to the Lord for allowing us to be blessed daily with her beauty, love, compassion, strength, courage, and wisdom.

As I reflect on the beauty of this entire journey, I realize that just as the seasons continue to change, I continue to become more "seasoned". In these moments of change I have learned to cherish what is important -- family, faith, hope and love but the one that gives me the most joy is love.

Shared Joy

Maurice K. Foushee

Shared Joy

Maurice K. Foushee

Calling all survivors! Survivors of health challenges, employment challenges, and those who have done their time and are living the retirement life. I share in the joy of your accomplishments; because while I can experience joy based upon my own personal achievements, I can experience it for you, too.

Being happy for yourself is not a selfish state of mind, but happiness just for yourself can make you an unsympathetic, self-satisfied, self-centered, and an obnoxious pain in the . . . aspiration. If you have ever felt as though any of these words could describe you or if you're feeling bored, unfulfilled, or noncommittal, maybe you are missing the joy that comes from being happy for others. I am happy for this opportunity to share some heartening or gratifying experiences that I have witnessed or supported, which eventually helped other people and me.

A great source of joy for me has been witnessing people's ability to, in some cases, tolerate a health concern, and in other cases completely conquer a chronic condition or life-threatening illness. I know people who have lost weight in a safe manner, or who no longer show diabetic symptoms, and who continue to eat healthy foods, exercise, or do both. Eating healthy foods and exercising might sound as if they should be automatic or easy habits to follow, but even for those of us who are relatively healthy, good eating and exercise actions and attitudes are not easy to achieve, especially long-term. "Slippin' into Darkness"

(1970's R&B fans of the singing group War will remember the title) can become more natural than achieving or maintaining good habits when you are battered by work and home obligations or convinced, or even deceived, by advertisements.

I have not forgotten the organ transplant patients I've known who had to wait on donation lists for years. Could I wait for years if I needed a transplant? I might if I did not have a choice, but I would probably worry one-half of my life away and rush through the other half. Yet, I have admired the generous and calm demeanor of people who have waited for transplants and their willingness to share and encourage others during and after their surgeries. Not just their physical victories, but their attitudes and testimonies impart joy because they show ways to conquer afflictions and attain or regain an attribute fading in so-called advanced cultures - patience.

Do you want another example of sharing selfless joy?

I am glad to see family, friends, and former co-workers change or improve their employment status. This is especially true for people who have been mistreated or unemployed, then later land a position where they are better treated, paid more, offered improved benefits, and can reduce their commute. Seeing these more confident and cheerful people is encouraging for anyone who might also experience a similar situation.

Did someone mention retirement?

Yes, I am even happy for those who retire - even while I wish I could do the same. C'mon retirement savings! C'mon retirement date! As much as I dream about, hope for, and plan for retirement and sometimes mess with retirees about returning to work, I am happy to see those good folks pursue old or new interests, spend time with people they care about, and connect with the world with a more relaxed attitude.

But what about me?

As much as I advocate sharing in the joy of others, having our own personal sources of joy is important, too. It's not selfish to find something you enjoy; I dare say that it is necessary. I have several hobbies that bring me joy and one of them is vocabulary building. Don't worry, I do have a few traditional and physical hobbies too; but learning the meaning and spelling of new words - please, no quizzes for me now - and using them correctly is a gratifying pastime.

Not every word I try to memorize has to be polysyllabic or, if you prefer, long. Some are just unique-sounding or uncommon words. Using unusual words occasionally, and only occasionally, with acquaintances can be a rare, amusing, and scholastic experience. Imagine going to a games party and dropping jewels such as, "Gail, I would not be mendacious if I told you that your choir sang in a mellifluous tone." or "I hope George will not become atrabilious or obstreperous if no one will volunteer to clean chitterlings for him." Before I move on, I will translate the two sentences into plain English: "Gail, I would not be lying if I told you that your choir sang in a sweet flowing tone." And "I hope George will not become sad or angry if no one will volunteer to clean chitlins for him."

Yes, vocabulary power is fun and is something I can share with a small circle of friends or family. Remember that while lifting word weights, no one wants to be bothered by a garrulous, grandiloquent arriviste who sends people into a state of apoplexy or just ennui. If you become this person, someone might try to extirpate you for being sententious. Just try to be sagacious and insouciant. Actually, what I intended to say was no one wants to be bothered by a talkative, pretentious social climber who sends people into a state of explosive anger or just boredom. If you become this person, someone might try to destroy you for being pompous. Just try to be wise and nonchalant.

Will I remember all of these words? No, but I will find joy in trying to learn them. Sometimes, the effort put forth for anything provides as much pleasure and feelings of achievement as the end of the trek. And equal joy is found when sharing this fun with others.

Yes, for me, the key to joy comes from sharing it. Joy shared is joy multiplied.

The Joy in Traveling

Dr. Katrina E. Miller

The Joy in Traveling

Dr. Katrina E. Miller

I am not sure when I first caught "the travel bug". It might have happened about the time I was six years old. That's my earliest recollection of our family vacations. My parents believed in family vacations. My father thought if you worked all year you needed to take some time off. I don't know where he got that philosophy from, but it's something that he instilled in me. Even as an adult he would ask me if I had planned some vacation time.

Our early family vacations were often trips to visit relatives in exciting parts of the country. To me, they were exciting and always filled with some great excursion. I remember one of our early trips to New York! We visited my uncle. It was so much fun staying in his one-bedroom apartment. We visited the Statue of Liberty, the Empire State Building, and Radio City Music Hall. Of course, a trip to Harlem was on the agenda, along with a visit to the Apollo Theatre. My young mind was overwhelmed by the bright lights and all the assortment of people. I have traveled to New York as an adult many times since then, but my first time there will always be special.

Our family vacations often took us to many of the New England states including Massachusetts, Pennsylvania, New Jersey and even Connecticut! Preparations and travel to these places where just as much fun as being there. We drove most of the time (traffic was not as bad as it is now) and my mother went to great lengths preparing us for all that we would see when we got there. As the trip organizer, my mother did the research regarding the tourist attractions for our city of choice. I think that might be how I got the job as trip planner when traveling with friends. I remember on the morning of our trip to Philly, she woke my brother and I up with one of her original songs. "We Going to Phila-delphia, We going to Phila-delphia". Of course, we visited the Liberty Bell and learned all about our nation's history. That was an unforgettable trip.

Once we drove all the way to Rochester, New York and then drove a few more hours to another country!! We were in Canada. I was so amazed that we could drive to another country. You know Niagara Falls was on the agenda for this trip. I remember journaling about the different sights I saw and comparing Canada to the United States. I was excited to return to school that year and respond to the all too familiar question, "What did you do last summer?"

We visited Disneyworld the year that it opened. I could not believe the heat and the fact that it would rain one minute and then the sun would come out the next. We also traveled to the Kennedy Space Center and Sea World. Universal Studios was not there yet, but don't worry, I have since traveled to Florida and experienced Universal Studios and all the newest Disneyworld attractions.

When my brother and I were teenagers, we took our first cross-country flight to California. (We were east coast babies.) During that trip we saw everything! So, I thought. Believe it or not we had west coast family and spent time with them. We went to Hollywood and to Universal Studios. While at Universal Studios, I was frightened by Frankenstein as we waited for our tour bus to leave and saw how "movie magic" was done. Compared to the special effects of today this was nothing. But to my young eyes, it was everything. We had a few celebrity sightings and enjoyed the ride to see the Sequoia trees. These redwood trees were much more plentiful than they are now.

Just like I remember these family trips, I also remember the last one we really took as a family. It was to Atlanta, Georgia. My brother and I were well into our teenage years and this was the summer before my senior year of high school. To say we were "smelling ourselves" is an understatement. While it was our usual family trip, complete with an itinerary, my brother and I were not having it. We spent much of that trip complaining about which phone calls we had missed from who and how our friends were at home in Maryland "living it up". You must remember this was well before cell phones and if you weren't at home, you would not be able to talk to your friends. On one particular complaint-filled day, my mother announced, "That's it, this is the last family trip we take" and by golly she meant that thing!

The summers to follow were filled with jobs and preparing for the fall semesters of college. Then, I graduated from college and a new level of "summer vacations" were born. These vacations were often taken with friends. These trips took on a different type of "flavor". My first adult trip was with my BFF to the Bahamas. Honey, you could not tell us we had not arrived. Thinking back, it was really a long weekend trip on then "Apple Tours". That first afternoon we could not believe our feet were in the waters of the Caribbean. We took a few tours, sat by the pool, and shopped. I still remember the big floppy hat I bought and all the Calypso cassette tapes I purchased. Since that initial vacation my BFF and I have climbed Dunn River Falls in Jamaica, visited the Pink Lake in Senegal, West Africa and seen the Door of No Return in Ghana. So many great memories that make my heart smile.

My first trip to Europe was a gift from my aunt when I completed my master's degree. She told me I would need a passport and couldn't believe how quickly I had gotten it (pre-911 it only took me 24 hours). My aunt had lived overseas for several years and knew all the places to visit. Of course I had done my own research and had a few places I wanted to experience. We flew first class to Paris. Yahoo! The memory of this trip is extra special to me.

Traveling soothed my soul when my mother passed away. A visit to Los Cabos, Mexico was just what my weary spirit needed. The warm breeze, calm waters, and welcoming citizens provided not only a memorable vacation but medicine for my soul. This prescription was repeated during the first Christmas without my father. A Christmas cruise took my brother, sister-in-law, and me away from wills, probates, and estate accounts. The celebratory atmosphere and delicious food on my first cruise provided a soothing place to calm my nerves.

On another note, travel has also served as a way to celebrate. I have used travel with my crew to celebrate birthdays, marriages, and divorces. I have discovered that people are more open to communication when away from home. Friendships have been rekindled and relationships reborn while on vacation.

I have been able to combine my love of travel with my profession. As a Speech Language Pathologist, travel has afforded me the unique opportunity to treat patients with communication disorders, to teach students from different cultures, and to train future practitioners in places all over the world.

Traveling has allowed me to shop in a variety of markets, malls, and specialized boutiques. I have taken trips in which the only purpose was to shop. Shopping has helped me to bond with family and friends. Shopping can also give one an open door to a variety of cultures and fashions. What shopaholic doesn't check out the most popular shopping spots in the cities they visit? The people I have met at international markets have been fascinating. Bonding over bargains is the fastest way to make friends and to have great conversations.

Finally, one of the greatest gifts travel has offered me is the chance to expand my mind and my point of view. Exploring different cultures and foods have put me at tables where I have learned how to use chop sticks, sampled fufu and jollof rice, and eaten food I wouldn't even look at if I was home. I have learned that people are really the same all over the world and that family is important, food is life, and just maybe there is another way to solve a problem or create a strategy.

So even if you aren't able to take that cruise or are hesitant to fly internationally, try a day trip or a visit to a tourist attraction in your hometown. It actually does not matter where you travel, just that you do it. Using a change in scenery to spark some joy is medicine for your soul.

The Joy of His Presence

Maria Miller Johnson

The Joy of His Presence

Maria Miller Johnson

As I look back over the years, I can see how the presence of God has continuously played a significant role in my life. My childhood, young adult, and now adult memories are full of countless encounters where His presence has led and guided me. Some of these experiences shook me to my core; but in the midst of them all, I've been blessed by the JOY and comfort of God's presence.

As a child, I knew about God. My family are Christians, and we were raised in the church. My parents took us to church every Sunday. On many Sunday mornings, my mother would prepare a hearty breakfast that included bacon, grits, eggs, fried apples, and toast. On other Sunday mornings she cooked our favorite, which included pancakes, bacon, and eggs. Once we finished our breakfast, we prepared for Sunday morning service.

The church we attended sang gospel music. I really enjoyed the praise and worship part of the service. It seemed as though that good old gospel music really spoke to my soul. I remember the choir singing, "Over my head, I see Jesus, Over my head, I see Jesus, Over my head I see Jesus, I see Jesus in the airrrr. There must be a God somewhere, there must be a God somewhere, there must be a God somewhere." I enjoyed clapping my hands and singing. I could really feel the presence of God. I would notice my family members were sitting in a more reserved posture. Maybe because their experience with church came from a more reserved posture. While I observed them, I asked myself,

"Don't they feel it, the presence of God?" Sometimes I would get so filled that I could feel tears streaming down my face. Just writing the words on this page brings tears to my eyes, for I am thankful that I recognize God's presence in my life.

There were other times during my childhood when I felt the presence of God, including visits with my maternal grandmother and paternal grandparents in North Carolina. My maternal grandmother was a prim and proper lady who loved God. During my visits with Grandma Connie, I have fond memories of her taking me to church, giving me my first children's Bible, and reading me Bible stories. I believe these times spent with her were some of my first introductions to God.

I also remember spending time with my paternal grandparents. They too were people who loved God and loved His Word. My grandfather, Isaac, was a deacon and my grandmother, Mary Elizabeth, was a faithful director and teacher of their children's church which they called the Sunshine Band.

These grandparents loved God and they lived by His Word. They were excellent teachers inside and outside of their home. As their grandchildren, we looked forward to our grandparents' Bible lessons and we definitely looked forward to the meals. My grandfather always had a garden and hogs. We looked forward to delicious homemade meals where the food came from their garden and the fresh meat from the hogs that my grandfather raised. Talk about an organic meal! Now that was organic eating. We all especially loved the homemade pancakes. I sure wish I had that recipe now. Enough of that, let me refocus. My paternal grandparents loved God's Word and they lived by God's Word. They would teach us Bible verses and read Bible stories to us.

It was a practice in their home that everyone would recite a Bible verse before each meal. So as young children they taught us verses, but as we got older, it was expected that we learn some on our own. One summer all ten of the grandchildren visited my grandparents at the same time. We were outside playing and having a good time. At some point my grandmother asked one of the children if they knew the Lord's Prayer and that child didn't know it. We all just looked at each other and knew play time was over. Mary Elizabeth said, "What? You don't know the Lord's Prayer? That's it! Everyone get in this house now. No one can go outside until everyone knows the Lord's Prayer. The older children must teach the younger children." Mary Elizabeth was serious about the Word of God and she wanted us to know the Word for ourselves. We all laugh about that experience now, but at the same time, it showed us how serious they were about not just knowing of God but truly knowing Him and his Word for ourselves.

I taught my children the Lord's Prayer and have taught it to my 6-year-old granddaughter, as well. I drive her to daycare each morning, and I decided to use our early morning commute as the time to teach her the Lord's Prayer and other Bible verses. While enroute to daycare, we pass a tree that my granddaughter calls the upside-down tree. When we reach that point every morning, she recites the Lord's Prayer. These experiences bring me tears of Joy to know that I can teach her prayer so she can get to know God for herself; and I pray that she will one day feel and appreciate His presence as much as I do.

In my young adult life, I attended and graduated from Bennett College and Howard University. I had been blessed with parents who paid for my undergraduate and graduate studies. So, I graduated from both College and University with no debt. Wow, that was a true blessing. I see how the Lord gave my parents opportunities to work so they paid for not only my advanced studies, but my two brothers' also. I do not take this for granted. I am very grateful for this.

After college, I married my college boyfriend and we had three beautiful children. My husband and I had so many similarities. We both had the surname Miller. We are not cousins. We both had several relatives with the same name, including our grandmothers who were both named Mary Miller. We both had uncles named David Miller who attended NC A&T. Both of our fathers were J. Miller and both attended NC A&T, as well. Some of our relatives attended A&T at the same time, a fact we discovered at our wedding.

Our mothers were both science teachers and they both taught at Martin Luther King schools, one in Washington, DC and the other in Maryland. My aunt and my mother-in-law had the same name and they both had mixed gray hair and had a family resemblance.

Our families not only had similarities in the family names, but the family values were similar, as well. Both were loving families that loved God. They each welcomed us into the respective families. I'd like to call this Divine Intervention and in it I found joy and felt the presence of God.

During the pregnancy with our second child, I experienced complications with the pregnancy. It was so serious that the doctors presented an option of abortion.

We were afraid but I was fixed and determined to believe God would heal our baby. I shared my situation with my faithful few prayer partners and with a coworker. My prayer partners prayed with me weekly and the coworker gave me the telephone number to a local church that had a prayer line. She said, all I had to do was call this number and there is a different prayer each day. So, I called every day of my pregnancy, and the message would say, hello friend and state a situation that spoke right to my circumstance every time I called. I was so surprised. It was like the Lord himself was talking right to me. I prayed that God would heal my child and that the baby would be healthy. The months went by and we delivered a healthy baby girl. Thank God for his presence in this situation. God used some praying friends and a kind coworker to stand in agreement with me and my family for a healthy baby. In fact, our marriage produced three healthy children who were all born in the same month. Two of them were born on the same day three years apart, and the oldest was born four days after the younger two. To God Be the Glory for the marvelous things He has done!

Several years went by and, as life would have it, my marriage ended. At that time, it was the worst thing that had ever happened to me. I was devastated. I wondered, "How did I get here? How will I care for myself and three young children?" I had never lived on my own. I quickly heard, "But God. Don't panic, it's a test."

I was an avid follower of Joyce Meyer's teachings. The television was on the morning I got the news of my divorce, and I heard her voice say, "Don't panic, it's a test." I stopped in my tracks and thought maybe it's a test and we will be able to restore the marriage. And maybe I'm being tested to see if I will keep moving and striving to do the things God placed in my heart to do.

I had a long-time desire to work as a therapist and to explore life coaching. You know how it is, it was one of those things on my to-do list that I just never got around to doing. Well, as life would have it, my long-time friend and mentor called me just at the beginning of my divorce process and shared that a woman down the hall from her office had opened a Life Coaching Institute and that we needed to sign up for her course. My response was, "Don't you know that I am going through a divorce? I have to pay this mortgage, daycare, etc. etc. etc." She insisted that we had to do this. Well, I thought about it, and I said to myself that this is the worst possible time in my life to get a Life Coaching Certification. But I also thought that this opportunity presenting itself now might be a sign that the devil doesn't want me to do this. So, I put on my big girl pants and said to myself what I taught my children to say, "I can do all things through Christ who strengthens me." The enemy doesn't want me to do this, so I have to manage my income appropriately and find a way to pay for the Life Coaching Certification.

I really wanted to do this, so I sold Mary Kay Cosmetics like I never sold Mary Kay before. I could not have my family saying I used money designated for household bills or my kids to pay for this course. And I did it. You can do a lot when your back is up against the wall and you turn to God for help. As it turned out, the benefits of that life coaching course were twofold; it helped me to cope with the divorce as I achieved my goal of getting the Life Coaching Certification. It helped me as I helped others. I also learned a lot about myself. I learned to enjoy my own company, to trust God and not man, and to try new things.

Now, on the other side of the divorce, I am grateful for the opportunity to coparent amicably, maintain a friendship with the family, and raise three beautiful children who love God. These are children who can have differing opinions but are able to put their differences aside and come together because they are family. Not all families have that kind of love for each other. That type of love only happens because of the presence of God in their hearts and that brings me Joy.

Another thing that has brought me a lot of joy during my adult years was learning how to run. I was not a very athletic person in school. I was the Pom-pom girl and the only running I did was in gym class. I could not run from my house to the end of the block. Nonetheless, during my time of newfound freedom and self-discovery, I learned how to run. My neighbor trained me to run a half marathon in 2009. I not only ran one half marathon, I did the Maryland Double. I ran two half marathons in the same year. My, that was an accomplishment and that experience really opened my mind to new and different opportunities. But most of all, it allowed me time to commune with nature and experience the presence of God at yet another level.

I recognize God's presence in my current relationship. I married a friend. My current husband and I participated in the same church Life Group and Bible study. I guess you could call it a divine appointment because, when he first came to the church, God pointed me out to him and told him that I would be his wife. When he heard that message from God, I was a greeter at the church, and I was welcoming him to the service. I was not thinking of him with any special interest. I was just welcoming him to the church. But God. It seemed other people knew that we would get married. Several people dreamt it.

My husband and I had only gone on one date and my cousin told me that I needed to get my house (business affairs) in order because he is coming. "He's tall and handsome", she said. I asked her, how she knew that. She said, it's that thing that Grandma had, a discerning spirit. She was right.

I recognized God's presence most recently during three family trips my two brothers and I were able to go on with our 80-year-old parents. We went to two Carolina Panthers games in Charlotte, North Carolina and one Dallas Cowboys game in Dallas, Texas. These three trips were priceless. This was the first time in forty years that our nuclear family had gone on a vacation together. We had been on trips with our parents that included our respective families, but not just with the nuclear family. It was great to be able to spend quality time together, watching the game, talking, dancing, and praying together. As my grandfather used to quote from the Bible, the effectual prayer of a righteous man availeth much.

As I look back over my life, I can see countless times, when I have found Joy in the Presence of God. Time and time again, God is always there to comfort me, keep me, lead, guide and direct me into His presence. I am grateful that I know Him and recognize the opportunities He has set before me. He says in His word, Be Still and know that I am God. It is in the stillness of His presence that I find Joy.

Embracing the Cycles of Life

Dr. Francina Moore Kerr

Embracing the Cycles of Life

Dr. Francina Moore Kerr

> *To everything there is a season, and a time for every matter or purpose under heaven. - Ecclesiastes 3:1*

It is said that our bodies, minds, and emotions go through a change every seven years. I can certainly attest to the truth in this statement as these past seven years have been transformative for me. As you might know, Biblically, the number seven often symbolizes completion or perfection. While I am not complete or perfect, I am striving towards perfection.

I would like to share parts of my past seven-year journey with you because I don't think most people are aware of the cycles our lives undergo. I don't want you to miss the transformative process that may be taking place in your own life.

The years 2015 to 2021 brought major changes that could be tagged as my "rites of passage" into the next season or cycle of my life. I am 79 years old and this recent 7-year cycle was just as important to me as the cycles I lived through during the earlier years of my life.

Annually, I identify four quadrants of my life that are important to me, and I set a goal in each of them. These quadrants are as follows: spiritual, physical, financial, and relational. Before solidifying them, of course, my goals are submitted to the Holy Spirit and bathed in prayer for direction and guidance. To ensure that I am reaching these goals, I review them periodically and make adjustments where necessary. I've noticed that in some years, there was not as much activity as in others, and you may notice the same thing.

2015—Release

This year was the beginning of a new seven-year cycle. Although I was still actively involved, both professionally and ministerially, I also felt unsettled, like it was time for something different. Perhaps this was the stirring to prepare me for releasing or better yet, shedding the old cycle and embracing the changes that were on the horizon.

2016—Restoration

During this year, I dreamed big time. The dreams were full of conflict and confusion. I think they may have been connected to the fact that I was in a situation that was not conducive for my growth. Can you relate to this? Has there been a time when you were stunted by something or someone who really had no place in your life?

On October 23, 2016, my dream was a request for a larger suitcase and that was BIG because it indicated that change was about to take place. The dream was interpreted as a private walk with God. The greater message was that God was moving me into a kingdom mandate.

This year posed more trips to the doctor than I have ever had in my entire life. Every month I had a medical appointment for something! The doctor surmised my health issues stemmed from stress rather than physical problems. With this knowledge, restoration was on the way. When I shared the dreams, instead of holding them in, all health issues subsided, as did the dreams.

2017—Connect the Dots

As I look back over this year, there were a lot of "endings". My connection to things that I had been attached to were severed as I recognized negative situations that I needed to set free. The apostolic word I received was "connect the dots!" As I saw it, the Holy Spirit was ending some things and replacing them with new opportunities; it was my job to follow the signs and "connect the dots." Only then would I be where God wanted me to be.

My prayer at the end of 2017 was, "Lord, in this season of my life, I need those people who will come alongside me to support me and help me to live a more joyous life. Help me to be sensitive to the directives (people, open doors) of the Holy Spirit and connect the dots as He leads."

2018—Freedom to "Be"

This was probably the quietest year of all. My husband of 47 years transitioned to glory in 2018. Thankfully, he made this time uncomplicated for us in that two years prior to his death, he had the children and me plan the details of his final days. We followed his instructions to completion and had a wonderful celebration of life that included his closest relatives and friends.

Afterwards I sensed a freedom to just "be." I began to explore new things and traveled a lot. It was also a year of questioning God regarding the "next season" of life. I still felt the need to be "doing" rather than "being". But God had other plans for His daughter! She still needed to "hear".

2019—Rest

I believe 2019 was the pivotal year in my seven-year cycle. You have to know that prior to this year, I was enduring a tremendous time of unrest, wanting more to "do" than to "rest". My life was so full of activities that I wasn't resting in God! What folk later said to me was, "you were all over the place." Mind you, I had been hearing the word "rest", but I couldn't receive it! Well, our Heavenly Father knows how to get our attention.

A friend of mine, who had relocated from Maryland to North Carolina, met a Christian educator and she said, "Fran, she is the epitome of you! You have got to meet her!" Well, if she was that much like me, you know I had to meet her.

It was the spring of 2019 when my friend told me about Dr. Iris Barrett, but I was not available to go to North Carolina until the fall. So, I scheduled a trip to Hickory, NC to attend her Bible study in September. Of course, we all introduced ourselves before the meeting started and at the close of the session, Dr. Barrett prayed for us individually. Before she got to me, I heard in my spirit, "rest". When Dr. Barrett got to me, she smiled and said, "Fran, the Lord says rest. He says, I've got you, I've always had you. Rest!" God spoke the word "rest" to my spirit from a source who knew absolutely nothing about me. I immediately received this word, and my life took on the mantle of "resting in God".

2020—New Beginning

At the end of 2019, I began to get a little uneasy during the winter months and felt the need to spend some time in a warmer climate.

Hence, I traveled to Newbury, Florida to spend a few months with my sister. During that time I kept hearing in my spirit, "I am the God of Abraham, Issac, and Jacob." I must say this was an intense time in study and staying in the presence of the Lord! I surfaced from this study knowing that God is the same yesterday, today, and forevermore. I learned that I must trust Him even when I could not trace Him.

To further strengthen my spirit and understanding of the Word of God, I took every free course Dallas Theological Seminary was offering. To exercise myself in the Word, I was asked to be the speaker for a monthly women's Bible study group. From that session, I have been asked to speak each year I am in Florida on a visit. Oh, what joy.

Upon my return to Maryland in June, I sensed a newness, a renewed sense of joy, which was evidenced by my environment -- totally decluttered, organized, and clean. There was also a sense of freedom in my spirit and in my relationship with God. Moreso than ever, I was hearing, knowing, and resting in Him. In other words, the Word of God became life to me. Additionally, there was a sense of physical well-being. While being in Florida, I had a membership at a health club that offered health and wellness training, both of which I took full advantage of.

And last of all, on September 6, 2020, someone whom I knew over 56 years ago re-entered my life. This person has helped me to see a side of life that I have never known before and it's beautiful! Someone said they felt God allowed me this experience. All that I accomplished in 2021 was undergirded by this experience. Where it is going from here, only God knows. In the meanwhile, I am following the yellow brick road.

2021—Transformation

Well, the end of my seventh year, 2021, was spectacular, over the top, and all encompassing! What God allowed me to experience and accomplish during that year in the four quadrants of my life brought joy to me beyond measure.

As I mentioned earlier, Biblically, the number seven often symbolizes completion or perfection. In that year, I reached a level of completion that catapulted me to another sphere or realm of being.

At the beginning of the year, I heard from several prophetic sources that God wanted His people to live a balanced life. This principle had been resonating with me for several years, but I had not heard it articulated as strongly in ministry circles as I was hearing it then. With that strong word, that I believed was truly from the Lord, I drew a circle that included the quadrants of life that were important to me and submitted them to the Holy Spirit's direction for what I considered "balanced living" for me. My operative Scripture for guidance was Proverbs 3:5,6, "Trust in the Lord with all your heart and lean not to your own understanding. In all your ways submit to Him, and He will make your paths straight." Included in the circle were my:

- Spiritual life

- Stewardship of my temple

- Stewardship of my finances

- Stewardship of my relationships

Spiritual Life

The core of my being, my foundation, is my relationship with God. So, for that year, I wanted to know God in a deeper way as my Heavenly Father. Without question, I believe COVID-19 placed all of God's children in a posture to spend more time with Him, enabling the Holy Spirit to redefine our relationship with Him from "church" to Kingdom. During the year, the rest and peace of knowing that God was in control of all things brought a sense of joy and comfort to my soul.

As I reflect over the past seven years, I can see the hand of God developing, training, and nurturing me in His character and attributes. I have sensed a settling or rest in my spirit of the faithfulness, care, protection, and guidance of the Holy Spirit. There has been a deeper communion in the Word, which became a living Word to me, as well as more fellowship in meditative prayer.

Stewardship of my temple

Again, a word that resonated in my spirit early 2021 was "God is raising up a people to carry the message of health, healing, and wholeness." If your ears are attuned to what the Spirit is saying today, you will hear this message being widely preached. In previous generations, attention was directed to developing our spiritual bodies with little to no concern for the temple that housed the spirit. As a result, we have birthed a generation of unhealthy, unwell, unwhole, sick people who are void of the happiness and joy they deserve. The message that we are hearing today is placing emphasis on health and wholeness. Just as we steward our finances and careers to be successful in life, we must also give the same time, attention, and discipline to our physical bodies. In addition to exercise, what we consume in food and drink is also important.

To steward my body, I have a personal trainer who challenges me three times a week with strength training exercises to help keep my physical body strong and flexible. Additionally, I have been blessed with a friend who is a registered nurse trained in nutrition. She keeps me on track to maintain healthy meals and eating habits. To this regimen, I have added a monthly massage to help remove stress and other toxins from my body.

Stewardship of my finances

My excitement is mounting here! I asked the Holy Spirit to help me devise a plan to eliminate my debt by the end of 2021. I was able to pay off three credit cards, as well as my car, and drastically lowered the interest rate on my home! What joy!

In addition, I'm truly grateful to God for a remarkable year of accomplishing some major updates to my home and all paid for! I was able to install new flooring, window dressings, appliances, and I had my home painted. Everything that I desired!! I have much to thank the Lord for!!!

Stewardship of my relationships

I purposed during 2021 to be more sensitive to the needs of others and how I could assist in meeting those needs. With that in mind, I engaged in community and fellowship with my family and those people in my circle of influence. In my interactions with them, I found myself to be more present, engaging, and non-judgmental. As a result, this created an atmosphere wherein they felt free to be open and honest in sharing what was on their minds. Additionally, being a good listener and actually hearing what was being communicated enabled me to discern how to respond, which blessed both me and the other person.

Now, don't think this seven-year cycle has been without its own set of problems and challenges. No, I didn't sail through them on a flowery bed of ease. During this time, I lost my husband of 47 years, my oldest and youngest sisters, a brother, two brothers-in-law, other relatives, and a host of very close friends. Closure had also come to other areas of my life that were very dear and meaningful to me. Yet, I had to come to the realization that there is a season and a time to every purpose under heaven. (Ecclesiastes 3:1).

I am grateful for the transformation that has taken place in me during these past seven years, and I look forward with tiptoe expectancy to what God is preparing for the next cycle. In the process, He has afforded me a measure of happiness and His joy has been my strength. Not only am I entering a new cycle, but I will also be adding a ZERO to the end of my age!

Blinded By the Blindness

Ernestine Williams

Blinded By the Blindness

Ernestine Williams

Summertime

It was a beautiful summer day; the sky was a magnificent shade of light blue and the clouds looked like fluffy white cotton balls. The year was 1970. I will not say how old I was, let's just say I was a little girl. I was eating my lunch with anticipation of the day's adventure with my grandmother.

During the summer my grandmother took me somewhere every day. Sometimes we'd go to the park or on a walk to the swimming pool. On Saturdays we often visited the library, and we would head straight for the children's reading room. There we would listen to a storyteller and then I got to pick out a book to take home. I had my own library card; you couldn't tell me nothing. Oh, and I failed to mention that we could end up at church, usher board meeting, or BTU (Baptist Training Union) on any day she felt that was necessary.

On one particular day I asked, "Where are we going today, Granny, are we going to the park?" She said "No, today we are going to the Blind Association." "The Blind Association?" I asked, "What is that?" She explained that it's a place where blind people go for support and to learn life skills. "Today we are going to be volunteers." "Me too?" I asked, "I'm going to be a volunteer, too?" "Yes," she said, "you are going to be a volunteer." Oh boy, I was excited! I did not know what a volunteer was but if Granny was going to do it, I knew that it had to be something good.

This was my introduction to blindness and to blind people; I was amazed at all the things that they were able to do without their eyesight. I had no idea how that experience would impact me later in life.

Emotional Blindness

On March 5, 1975, when the school bus pulled up to the bus stop, I was so excited to see that my mother was waiting for me. Usually, Granny picked me up at the bus stop, but if Mommy had the day off, she would come to get me off the bus. I got off the bus and threw my arms around my mother. She gave me a big hug and asked me how my day was. "Good!" I replied as we walked toward home. I asked her "Did you have the day off?" She said no, but that she had left work early. "Yay I'm happy to see you." Then I asked, "Where is Granny?"

My mother became quiet and just kept walking. I asked again, "Is Granny at home?" Finally, she explained, "No, Granny got sick today and had to go to the hospital."

"Oh", I said "she will be all right, when can we go to see her?" We were home by this point, so we sat on the porch steps. My mother said we would not be going to see Granny because she went to heaven. I said, "You mean she died?" My mother said "yes, your grandmother died today."

That was the day I first experienced what I call "emotional blindness" to describe my feelings or emotions. I was numb. It was if my emotions had blacked out. I was so sad when my grandmother passed away. Although there was nothing physically wrong with my eyesight, I could not see through my sadness. I was young and had not experienced grief. Seeing how strong my mother was during that time made me think about how much I loved and missed my grandmother. My mother had to be going through because her mother had died. I remember thinking then about how sad she must be, but somehow she was seeing her way through it, and so would I.

Blindsided

I had a wonderful childhood. My parents were great. I had everything I needed. I had a lot of friends and did fairly well in school. My love for theater and the preforming arts grew during high school. I did a lot of community theater and I sang with the youth choir at church.

All was well until our family was blindsided by the death of my father. How could this be happening?

It was the end of my junior year of high school. No one saw that coming. It was very sudden, unexpected, and very sad. This time I had to be strong for my mother who had become a widow; and for me, the grief was real and overwhelming. But God made a way. I graduated from high school the next year and went to college. I earned a Bachelor of Fine Arts degree from Howard University, a Bachelor of Education from Medaille College in Buffalo NY, and a Master's in Organizational Leadership from Nyack College in Washington DC. Once again all was well.

Then, on April 3, 2004, the Lord called my dear mother home. This grief was unbearable. I was emotionally blinded with sadness, sorrow, and grief. I was blindsided by life. Without my mother I was totally lost, but I kept moving forward as I knew she would want me to do.

The following year, I took a teaching job in Prince George's County,

Maryland where I taught elementary school.

Blinded by the Blindness

It was Labor Day weekend 2014, the end of the summer and the beginning of the next school year. I decided to prepare one of my favorite meals -- crab legs, baked potato, and salad. It had been an extremely hot day, so I waited for the sun to go down so I could enjoy my dinner on the balcony. I was enjoying my meal when my right eye started to itch. I rubbed it and did not think anything about it. After all, it was summer, I have allergies and I was sitting outside. My eye began to itch again, but this time when I rubbed it, my right eye went dark. I wasn't quite sure what was happening, but then I covered my left eye and I could not see a thing. Everything was black.

I went to the emergency room and was seen by one doctor after another, yet no one could tell me what the problem was or what to do about it. The bed I was on was rolled into the hallway where there were many other people waiting to be seen. There was not enough space in the emergency room, so they just rolled people to the hall to wait. I laid out there for twelve hours. I was not in any pain, but the sights and sounds in that hallway were unnerving. People all around me were screaming and crying out in pain, while new arrivals were being brought in by ambulance with all kinds of injuries and problems. Finally, I was admitted to a room and sent for an MRI on my brain. I had a book in my purse, so I started to read while I waited for the results of the test. I kept telling myself that I cannot be going blind because I was reading the book simply fine. It was late, so I figured I would not get the results from the test until the morning. I made phone calls to let a few people know where I was. I said my prayers and tried to sleep.

The first people I saw the next morning were the doctor and his team of residents. They had come to tell me that the MRI revealed there was a mass on my brain. "Mass on my brain" I replied, "what are you talking about?"

The doctor said "Ms. Williams you have been diagnosed with a brain tumor." I thought to myself "Oh my God I have brain cancer!" It was as if the doctor was reading my mind or maybe it was the expression on my face. He quickly explained, "Oh no, no Ms. Williams, the mass is benign, there is no cancer." I felt so much relief and joy in that moment that I forgot all about my eyesight. I was thankful and I am sure I said thank you to Jesus. He said the neurosurgeon would be there shortly to talk to me about the surgery. "Oh Lord what surgery?", I wondered.

The neurosurgeon came and explained to me that the tumor was resting on my optic nerve, that's why there was loss of sight in my right eye and brain surgery was necessary to remove the mass to save the sight in my other eye. Yikes BRAIN SURGERY!

The idea of surgery was unsettling, but I was not afraid. For God hath not given us the spirit of fear; but of power, and of love, and of a sound mind 2 Timothy 1:7. I knew that the God who spared my life would give me the power and sound mind to overcome the obstacles that I would have to face. My life would be forever changed. I was blinded by blindness.

Legally blind was the diagnosis, with no sight in my right eye and limited vision in my left. This meant I was disabled; I didn't know which was worse; being legally blind or emotionally blindsided by the whole situation. I had a long road ahead of me.

The next six months were extremely difficult. I had to recover from the surgery, I had to quit my job, and I had to literally figure out what my life was going to look like. Without a job how was I supposed to live, eat, or keep a roof over my head? I was emotionally drained and depressed but, spiritually, I knew I had the power to overcome my problems. When worry ends faith begins and II Corinthians 5:7 says "we walk by faith not by sight." This Bible verse would become a lifelong affirmation for me and start the journey toward reclaiming my joy.

After I recovered and was well enough to go out, the first place I headed was to church choir rehearsal and then to Sunday morning worship service. Just being in the house of the Lord and giving thanks for all He had brought me through, felt like a load had been lifted from my shoulders. It just confirmed my affirmation that I was ready to walk by faith and not by sight. I am so grateful to my Pastor and the support of my church family, as well as the help I received from my caregiver who is one of my oldest and dearest friends.

I had to figure out how I was going to live and survive as a blind person. On paper I am legally blind, but I identify as visually impaired. Whatever the label you put on it, I knew it was time for me to escape the emotional blindness and reclaim the joy that had been my life. I knew it could be done because, thanks to my grandmother, I had been exposed to blind and visually impaired people and the fond memories of volunteering at the Blind Association. I just needed to find the right support systems to help me adjust to my vision loss. The National Federation for the Blind helped me to do that.

One of my biggest problems was that everything was dim, and in some cases everything was dark. Everywhere I went I just felt like saying

"Will you turn on the lights please?", but the lights were on. Soon I took some mobility classes that taught me how to use a white cane to assist me with walking and crossing the street. I also learned other skills to help with daily tasks.

A friend of mine suggested I contact the Department of Rehabilitation Services to see if they could help me to get on track with a new career path. They referred me to The Business Enterprise Program for The Blind. This is a nationwide program that prepares blind or visually impaired individuals to operate retail concessions, gift and food service businesses in public facilities. Now this would be a faith walk because I had not foreseen such a life change. I was accepted into the program and completed the course work, which was not easy. I graduated from the Maryland State Business Enterprise Program for the Blind in 2016 and became a licensed manager.

I am currently the owner/manager of a snack shop in a federal building in Maryland. Just when I thought doors would be closing in on my professional life, a whole new door opened in entrepreneurship. I can truly say I have been walking by faith and not sight, and by doing so the Lord's vision has afforded me the opportunity to reclaim my joy.

Hidden Joy

Minister Shuwanda K. Williams

Hidden Joy

Minister Shuwanda K. Williams

Tuesday started out like any other day of the week in the life of a certified public accountant (CPA) during tax season; meetings all day--morning, afternoon, and evening. I had just finished my first morning meeting (an easy discussion with a recurring client) and was waiting for my 1:00pm appointment with a new client. In the meantime, my office assistant informed me that my 5:00pm appointment called to reschedule because he had to work late. With that evening cancellation, I was looking forward to a free afternoon to review returns and then going home early!

My 1:00pm appointment arrived early, around 12:40, so I had my assistant put the client in our conference room. During this time of year I needed every moment I could get, so I wanted to use this extra 20 minutes wisely to get some other work done. I entered the conference room at the scheduled time and saw this elderly woman with her daughter. As she greeted me, I immediately discovered from her accent that she was Jamaican. She managed to give a slight smirk, like a half smile. Behind that smirk this lady with a deep tan complexion and silver fox hair was gorgeous. She was dressed to the T! Although she was frail, she looked fabulous, especially for an 87-year-old woman. I will refer to her as "Ms. J". Her daughter, on the other hand, was a 55-year-old registered nurse who had just come from work and was still in her work clothes. The daughter's tone was quite different from her mom's, and it was obvious to me that she was the one in control! She was the boss!

After the introductions, we got down to business. The daughter began to tell me that her father died the prior November and he had always taken take care of the finances and taxes. Her mother, now a widow, was never involved with the finances. The woman knew her husband always dabbled in investments and the stock market but was unclear about exactly what he was doing. She did know, however, that he kept much of the paperwork in two envelopes that he kept in a particular bag, and he told her that if anything ever happened to him, to take this bag full of information to the "right" person.

As the mother pulled two large, stuffed, gold manila envelopes from the bag, and sat them in the middle of my conference room table, I could tell that her countenance began to change. We were strangers. She nor her daughter knew me, and I did not know them. I immediately determined that whatever was in those envelopes was very important. Those envelopes held some of her husband's most prized possessions. I could see the fear coming over Ms. J's face. It was if she was asking herself, "Can I trust her with my husband's golden bag? Can I share with her the details of his lifelong hobby? Is she the 'right' person that my husband talked about?"

I knew that she was having doubts about letting me see what was in those envelopes and that if we were to work well together, I had to gain her confidence. So, I decided to change the conversation away from the finances and to talk about her husband. I said to her, "Your husband must have been a wonderful man, please tell me something about him." Well, it was as if I opened up Pandora's box! Her countenance immediately began to change. She told me the story about how they met and fell in love during their teenage years, how they married, started a family, and moved to this country for a better life for their family. She talked about how they had jobs with the federal government, but her husband had a knack for finances and taught himself about the stock market and finances in his spare time. Her face beamed as she talked about how they traveled throughout the years to many countries and visited relatives in Europe and Canada. She called him her "sweetie". They had built a beautiful home in Washington, DC and even owned some rental properties. She talked about how they did everything together. If you saw one of them, the other one was only a footstep away, she explained. By this time, she was laughing, telling stories about their families, and reminiscing about what a wonderful man she had. She said, "He is not here now, but I find my greatest joy in the memories we made and that keeps me going. I have joy in my soul!"

It was in that moment I began to reflect on what "real" joy is. You see, this event happened at a tough time in my life--six months after a divorce from 21 years of marriage. I really did not feel like there was any reason for me to be joyful. However, seeing this woman transform as she reflected on the one thing that made her happy -- just witnessing her inner joy--was utterly amazing. This day was so magical, and I believe she was God's gift sent to help me see joy with new eyes. This lady had lost her partner of fifty plus years, yet she chose not to focus on her loss. Instead, she chose to face her tomorrows with the memories of joyful times.

The three of us were so engaged in her storytelling that we did not notice that an hour and a half had passed. Suddenly, Ms. J. pushed the two gold envelopes in front of me and said, "I need you to look inside." That meant I had passed the test. I was indeed the "right" person.

The envelopes were stuffed with all types of original stock certificates --General Motors, Exxon, Walt Disney, General Electric, and the list can go on and on. Some of the Walt Disney stock certificates were in color and dated back to the 1950's. I also saw coupons for bearer bonds, and this was overly concerning. Given my background as a CPA, I quickly realized that anyone could attach their names to these bonds and claim them. Wow! It hit me like a ton of bricks. I was holding original stock certificates and bonds that had never been recorded with a brokerage house for safe keeping. What should I do next? I told them that I needed to call my financial advisor for help.

My first thought was to immediately get this information recorded with a brokerage company. Trying not panic, I called one of my financial advisors and explained the situation. He panicked too. Ironically, he had just finished a meeting and was only about 15 minutes from my office. Thank you, Lord!

As he entered my conference room, I made all the introductions and told the mother and daughter that I had full confidence in this advisor. The financial advisor, I will call him "Mr. Miracle", informed them of the seriousness of this situation. He had to take an inventory of all the certificates, price them at today's market value and take all the paperwork to his brokerage company. The mother and daughter agreed, and he used the next hour and a half to cautiously price out those certificates on his laptop.

All three of us anxiously awaited as he worked. "I am finished," said Mr. Miracle. "Ms. J, I want to let you know that you are the proud owner of stocks and bonds totaling $1.5 million dollars." We were amazed. There really was a pot of gold in those gold envelopes!

We all had to take a minute to absorb what had just happened. By now, it is about 4:30pm and the financial advisor had to get this information recorded. He called the central office of his brokerage company and was informed that Ms. J. had to sign some paperwork in the DC office. He was kind enough to take the mother and daughter to the office to see this transaction through completion.

Before heading out, Ms. J. looked at me with a big smile on her face and said, "You were my angel, you were the right one!" With a smile of immense joy on her face, she said, "My sweetie is still looking out for me!"

I honestly believe that my encounter that day was a divine appointment. Although she came to me to help her, I was the real victor that day because she helped me re-examine the true meaning of joy when I needed it the most. Ms. J. was now a millionaire; however, her real wealth was not in dollars and cents, but her real joy was the hidden joy of her heart.

Joy is a condition of the heart. Joy is not a feeling. Joy is a fruit of the Spirit. According to the Bible, it is the second fruit of the Spirit.

But the fruit of the Spirit is love, joy, peace, longsuffering, kindness, goodness, faithfulness. Galatians 5:22

Many confuse the terms happiness and joy. These two are not interchangeable. In the Greek, the word for joy is "chara." This describes a feeling of inner gladness, delight, or rejoicing. This inner gladness leads to a cheerful heart and a cheerful heart leads to cheerful behavior. Joy is from within, regardless of what is going on around you!

Happiness is an emotion--an outward expression--and God never intends for people to be in that emotional state all the time. For Ecclesiastes 3:4 tells us that there is a time to weep, and a time to laugh; a time to mourn, and a time to dance.

A common mistake we often make is to think that getting something will make us happy. We tell ourselves, if only... if he would leave, if she would leave, if the children would leave, if I got married, if I got divorced. We want a life full of fun, full of bliss, a sense of self-fulfillment, and void of any problems.

Instead of chasing happiness, we ought to seek joy. After all, the Bible speaks much more about joy than about being happy. While happiness is a glad feeling that depends on something good happening (like a job promotion or winning the lottery), joy can be felt regardless of what we're going through.

When we view the instability of the economy, the uncertainty of our government, and the worldwide pandemic, it may seem difficult to be joyful. Our lives have changed, and we are facing adversity that is unprecedented. But Ms. J. (or Ms. Joy) helped remind me that true joy comes from filling one's spiritual void with true relationships, primarily a relationship with the One who provides pure joy – Jesus Christ.

Being united with Jesus Christ is the source of our joy. Where Christ and His kingdom are present; joy is present. God wants us to experience happy times, but His greatest desire is that you and I have unconditional joy.

Jesus said His joy would "remain in you" - John: 15:11- These things I have spoken to you, that My joy may remain in you, and that your joy may be full. and "your joy no one will take away."

We can have life when we know joy, choose joy and live joy!

Meet the Presenter

Gail Clanton

Gail Clanton is president of Clanton Communications, LLC a full-service writing and publishing company located in the Washington, DC area.

She is the author of the Amazon best-seller, *Sparkle In The Rain*, and her writing has appeared in *The Black Woman's Book of Travel and Adventure, Our Fathers Which Art in Heaven, Women Inspiring Nations*, and in the first volume of *Living In The Key of Joy*. She is a ghostwriter and also blogs at diaryofagrownupchurchgirl.com.

As a professional writer and editor, Clanton leads writing workshops designed to help people embrace the value of their stories and to more fully recognize the power of their words.

As a speaker, she shares with groups of all sizes from her own experiences, while revealing the strategies she uses to keep her own joy and sparkle intact.

And as a certified professional life coach and a Christian life coach, Clanton helps adults get in touch with their own internal power source so that they gain more complete happiness, success, and joy.

She holds a MA in Journalism from the Philip Merrill School of Journalism at the University of Maryland, College Park.

Clanton can be reached via her website, Gailclanton.com.

Made in the USA
Middletown, DE
19 August 2022

70703467R00077